Listening to the Animals

LOVING THE CHILDREN

EDITED BY PHYLLIS HOBE

A GUIDEPOSTS BOOK

ACKNOWLEDGMENTS

Every attempt has been made to credit the sources of copyrighted material used in this book. If any such acknowledgment has been inadvertently omitted or miscredited, receipt of such information would be appreciated.

"For a Child's First Pet," by Joanna Emery, "Funeral Prayer," by Dean Tolman, "Three Little Fish," by Cheryl Morikawa, "The Animals Never Yell at Me," by Michael, and "Old Friends," by C. David Hay, are from *Animal Blessings,* edited by June Cotner. Published by HarperCollins Publishers. Copyright © 2000 by June Cotner.

"Skippy," by Crystal Ward Kent, is used by permission of the author.

"A Lapful of Love," "Loving Again" and "Sweetie Pie," by Nancy B. Gibbs, are used by permission of the author.

"A Purrfect Pet Project" and "Pepper Catches the Burglars," by Roberta Sandler, are used by permission of the author.

"The Cuckoo," by Victoria Ries, is used by permission of the author.

"The Old Red Barn" and "My Bestest Friend," by Mary M. Alward, are used by permission of the author.

"Quacky," by Thelma Taylor, is used by permission of the author.

"Sammy," by Kevin Glaesman, is used by permission of the author.

"Security," by Jessie Eyer, is from *Animal Stories by Young Writers,* edited by William Rubel and Gerry Mandel. Published by Tricycle Press. Text copyright © 2000 by The Children's Art Foundation.

"My Friend Bob," by Diane M. Ciarloni, is used by permission of the author.

"From Terror to Trust," by Ed Eames, is used by permission of the author.

"A Dog's Life," by Bea Sheftel, is used by permission of the author.

"When Barney Disobeyed," by Byron M., and "A Spark of Life," by Brad Steiger and Sherry Hansen Steiger, are from *Animal Miracles,* by Brad Steiger and Sherry Hansen Steiger. Published by Adams Media Corporation. Copyright © 1999 by Brad Steiger and Sherry Hansen Steiger.

"Rite of Passage," by Brenda Randolph, is used by permission of the author.

"A Cat Named Hope," by Dee Sheppe, is from *Cat Caught My Heart,* by Michael Capuzzo and Teresa Banik Capuzzo. Published by Bantam Books. Copyright © 1998 by Michael Capuzzo and Teresa Banik Capuzzo.

"Goldie, the Peking Drake," by Evelyn v. K. Benham, is used by permission of the author.

"The Wisdom of Athena," by William Hendryx, is from *Woman's Day,* March 12, 1996.

(continued on page 208)

Designed by SMS Typography
Illustrations by Michelle Lester
Jacket designed by Dennis Arnold
Printed in the United States of America

Contents

DEVOTED COMPANIONS

READY TO HELP

SHARING THE FUN

LESSONS WE REMEMBER

Introduction

If you were to ask me, I could name every animal who has been a part of my life. I could even tell you stories about each of them and what they meant to me. No two were alike, and I loved each of them for what they were: my dearest friends. They still are, even though many of them are long gone.

The love between an animal and a child is very special. The child is new to the world, and the animal is new to the environment in which it finds itself. They grow up together, but at a different pace. The animal grows much faster because its time on earth is shorter. But there is much it can teach the child, and so their days are filled with learning—but in the sweetest ways.

In LOVING THE CHILDREN, one of Guideposts' exclusive series, *LISTENING TO THE ANIMALS,* some exceptional writers bring you true stories of the special relationship between animals and children. In the first chapter, *Just Being Together,* we share the joy they find in each other. Joanna Emery's prayer, "For a Child's First Pet," describes the hope and expectation every parent has for this first meeting. Then Crystal Ward Kent tells us about "Skippy," the dog she wanted for such a long time, the one she thought would be with her forever. Roberta Sandler, on the other hand, didn't want any more animals, but what could she do when her daughter seemed to attract them?

The stories in *Devoted Companions* describe the influences of our animal friends as children grow up. Nancy Gibbs introduces us to Sweetie Pie, the cat who helped her college-age daughter achieve independence. In "A Dog's Life," Bea Sheftel remembers her dog, Chrissy, who was her single mother's nanny for her children. In a remarkable story, "From Terror to Trust," Ed Eames tells us about Perrier, his guide dog, and his granddaughter who was terrified of him.

In our third chapter, *Ready to Help*, we meet some animals who get us through the hard times. For instance, in "A Cat Named Hope," by Dee Sheppe, a shelter cat who needed a home helps a young boy deal with rejection. In "Goldie, the Peking Drake," by Evelyn v. K. Benham, a duck finds a way for an overburdened mother to keep a rambunctious little boy safe. Mary Jane Stretch's story, "The Kiddos," is a touching example of young people and animals helping each other.

Sharing the Fun, our fourth chapter, is just that—fun! Sharon Huntington's story about "The Submarine," a strange piece of abandoned equipment she and her brother found on their grandparents' farm, is pure pleasure (bees and all!). In "Mockingbird Summer," Larry Habegger will enchant you with memories of that spectacular bird, and the effect it had on his life. And Kathryn Lay touches our hearts with "Memories With Mitzy," the kitten who reunited her with her girlhood friend, Belinda.

In *Lessons We Remember*, we look back to the animals who helped to shape our lives. The stories are sad, yet beautiful. Francyne Anderson describes her part-Scottish terrier, Pat, who looked after her family, even to the point of patrolling the streets around their home. In "An Answered Prayer," Christie Craig describes her disappointment when her parents gave her an iguana instead of a puppy or a kitten—and then her surprise at finding what a wonderful friend she had. And Mary Chavoustie's story, "A Time for Love," will warm your heart as you read about the castaway dog who helped a family deal with their grief—and who, incidentally, is the dog on the jacket of this book.

So many of us can look back fondly and relive the times we have spent with the animals of our childhood. They were good times, and we thank God for them. Our animal friends will never leave us, and we thank God for sending them to us in the first place.

PHYLLIS HOBE

LOVING THE CHILDREN

JUST BEING TOGETHER

---

*"Blessed are You, Lord God,
for all living creatures
You have made."*

ANTOINETTE HOLT

The animals in our lives don't ask very much of us. They simply enjoy being with us, no matter what we may be doing. This is an art—perhaps we ought to learn how to practice it. Imagine feeling that the world is a good place to be, just because you're with a friend. You don't have to do anything or say a word. Being you, being there, is enough.

For a Child's First Pet

JOANNA EMERY

$\mathcal{M}$ay this little pet bring pleasure and make the
cloudiest days seem bright

May this little pet bring comfort and warmth when
the world feels cold and lonely

May this little pet teach patience and caring—
foundation of all earthly peace

May this little pet foster understanding through
the universal language of life and love

May this little pet grow along with this child from
season to season and year to year

May this little pet create love everywhere through
its sheer being in our lives

from ANIMAL BLESSINGS

Skippy

CRYSTAL WARD KENT

$\mathcal{S}$he was the dog of my childhood, coming to me when I was five years old. I had long dreamed of a puppy, and pleaded with my parents all that year. My father teased me, asking numerous questions about my dream dog. "What kind do you want? What would you call it? What would you do with a puppy, anyway?" he would say. I answered at length, sure that a puppy was in the offing, but months passed and none appeared.

Then, one fall afternoon, I sensed something was up. I came home from kindergarten, and found my grandmother there to stay with me. My mother and my great aunt had to do a mysterious errand in a neighboring town. Mom rarely went off right after school, and from their twinkling eyes and barely contained smiles, I sensed this was no normal excursion. My grandmother bustled me into the kitchen for a snack, and they left.

I was sipping my milk when it hit me. A puppy! Maybe at last I was getting a puppy! I confronted my grandmother. "It's a dog, isn't it?" I said.

"A dog! I doubt it!" grandmother replied. "Maybe a hot dog. Your mother has her hands full with you and your baby sister without having a puppy underfoot. Now, finish your cookies!"

But the feeling that my dream was coming true persisted, and I could hardly wait until they got home.

Auntie and my mom were in high spirits as they set out to town, so much so that when they encountered my great-aunt Marion, they invited her along, too. No one can resist puppies, and I now had a committee out to select my first dog. Their destination was Newbury's Department Store, where a litter of puppies was for sale at five dollars apiece. They were Collie-Shepherd crosses, chubby and playful. Each dog was adorable, but my two aunts and my mom sought that something special that every first dog should have. "This one!" Auntie said, without hesitation. "There's a sweetness to her face." And so the department store dog came home to me.

I don't remember much about our first meeting. It was a blur of excitement, squeals, hugs, and the puppy peeing on the floor. All I know is I looked at her and she looked at me, and we knew we were friends. I decided to call her "Skippy" for no other reason than I liked the sound; it seemed fun and happy, and I knew that's how we would be together.

Despite her parentage, Skippy's ears lay silky and flat; her coat was long like her Collie ancestor, and she had a beautiful white ruff and four white paws. Her face was also more like a Collie's, with the longer nose and white markings around her eyes and muzzle. But her dark caramel coat was streaked with black, following her German Shepherd blood. She was a striking dog from the start.

She spent her first night in a basket with a blanket, a warm water bottle, and a clock. My mom knew what would happen if she was allowed to sleep in my room—one cry and she'd be in the bed. Still, I checked on her numerous times, and neither one of us slept much that first night.

During the next few weeks, my mother began the challenge of housebreaking Skippy. She encouraged her to do her business by the evergreens at the edge of our field. Skippy learned quickly, but her intelligence nearly proved her undoing. About a month after her arrival, a hurricane bore down on our region. The wind was already gusting hard when we took her out for her last bathroom call before "battening the hatches." Mom and I were running around picking up items in the yard when we noticed Skippy. She had headed toward the field to go and the wind blasting across the open area was nearly blowing her away. She was literally hanging on with her toenails! I rushed down, scooped her up, and we headed in.

Skippy was my first responsibility. She was a dear living creature that needed my care, and I was awestruck at the importance of my role in her life. I fed her, filled her water dish, and brushed her long coat. My parents stressed the importance of having a well-trained dog, and helped me teach her basic commands. During our early sessions, I had visions of dog shows and blue ribbons, but since none of these were available to dogs of mixed pedigree, I contented myself with the knowledge that my dog was smart and minded well. Or, minded well up to a point.

Skippy was beautifully trained, even following hand signals, until the day Mugsy moved in next door. Mugsy was the naughty friend that every child—and every dog—encounters sooner or later. He blissfully ignored all calls to come, barked constantly, and used every trick in his arsenal to lure Skippy over the wall to play. Mugsy also roamed the neighborhood at will, and was prone to chasing anything in sight—cats, birds, wildlife—and cars. To my fear and dismay, Skippy began picking up this last bad habit, and soon she had to be tied, save for when she played with me. One day, while we played, a car started up down the street. Ignoring my calls, Skippy hurtled after it, but she misjudged and the car knocked her down. The distraught driver leaped out, and my dad, hearing the screech of tires, rushed out the door. I stood there, fist in my mouth, too scared to even cry. My beautiful Skippy lay still, her head bloodied.

"It's alright," my dad said to the driver, as he picked up my dog. "She ran right in front of you. It's not your fault." He carried Skippy to the house, and as we reached the door, her eyes opened. "She's alive!" I cried, but my dad was still concerned so we took her to the vet's. The vet pronounced her concussed, but otherwise okay. "She's a very lucky dog," he said. "Give her some aspirin and keep her quiet—and keep her away from the road."

The car incident seemed to cure Skippy of her taste for automotive game, and our carefree lives resumed.

Skippy was my first best friend. During those early years, my sister was still too young to be much of a playmate, and there were no other children in the neighborhood. I had been a bit lonely, but now all that changed. After school, as soon as I was off the bus, we were off to the field or the woods, two explorers on new adventures. We discovered the four trees that made a secret playhouse, found a big rock perfect for picnics, and examined the wonders of our pond. We tracked toads and frogs and snakes, and other creatures unknown. Sometimes we just sat and watched the clouds or the bugs flying about. I can still feel her warm coat under my arm, and smell the summer grass. I remember that feeling of time stretching out forever.

Later, other children moved into the neighborhood, and Skippy and I were soon back and forth to their houses. My loneliness was gone, and I felt that I knew my place in the world.

When I was 10, we noticed something wrong with Skippy. A small bunch had formed at her throat, and she began to have trouble swallowing. She was now five, and the vet thought it was a fatty tumor, an ailment common in middle-aged dogs. He gave her some injections, and she seemed to improve. For awhile, everything was back to normal, but it was only a reprieve. Two months later, all her old difficulties returned. She also tired easily and seemed in pain. One day, she couldn't get up. We called the vet, and Skippy was scheduled for exploratory surgery on Monday.

That day was the longest of my young life. Somehow I got through school. All I wanted was to see my beloved dog again. But it was not to be. Dear Skippy had cancer, and the kindest thing had been to not revive her from the anesthesia. My great-aunt held me while I wept my heart out. "Why, why, why!" was all I could say. My best friend had been ripped from my life. I was alone and adrift again.

Skippy was cremated and buried beneath the evergreens she loved. My first dog was also my first experience with the death of someone close to me. I had prayed, yet my prayers had not been answered—at least not in the way I hoped. I did not understand, and that haunted me as much as her death. Auntie tried to comfort me.

"You prayed for her to live, but how do you know that she wasn't pleading for an end to her pain?" she said. "Would you have wanted her to survive but suffer? I believe God saw a chance to ease a good animal's suffering and took her home with him. You had her for five wonderful years. Be happy with that; remember that always, and be grateful that now she is at peace."

Her words did not make an impression right away. I was too miserable for them to penetrate. I couldn't bear to be with the other kids and their dogs, and the woods, once my refuge, now held too many sad memories. But gradually, like rain on stone, Auntie's message wore through my sadness. The day did come when I could think of Skippy without sadness, when I could laugh at stories of her antics, and remember so many good times.

Later that year, I wrote a composition about Skippy for a school writing assignment. It told of how she barked at ginger ale, and scolded my dad for trimming her beloved evergreen trees. I wrote of her love for Dad's old black truck, and her keen awareness of correct driving speed. If he exceeded 45 miles per hour, she placed her paw gently but firmly on the steering wheel, instructing him to slow down. She also barked at any cars that passed us. I'm not sure if we were just supposed to be in the lead, or she was warning them about high speeds.

As I wrote, so many memories poured forth. Years and years of them. Skippy and I floating on the raft at the lake; the way the sun turned her coat to burnished copper; her gentleness with Auntie, who could walk her on a string! I remembered her spell of kleptomania, when mysterious gifts began to appear on our doorstep—slippers, a dry mop, a floral arrangement—all pilfered from around the neighborhood, even from the cemetery! The thievery ended when she tried to give some "hot loot" to Auntie, who commanded, "Skippy, take that back!" Skippy did, and never stole again.

As I wrote, something inside me melted, and I knew I was healed. I would miss Skippy all my life, but I was now ready to make new friends and move on.

Many years have passed since my time with Skippy, yet she

is always with me. It is her picture I keep on my bedroom shelf, and I still have her dog tags in a heart-shaped box. When I walk in the woods, her spirit is there, still keeping pace with me just as she did when I was a lonely child. She was the dog of my childhood, and thanks to her love and companionship that became a golden time. She taught me about love and loyalty and friendship, and when it was time, she taught me about loss and letting go. She taught me about life, and that is her greatest gift of all.

A Lapful of Love

NANCY B. GIBBS

"I have something for you, honey," my father exclaimed as he came into my bedroom. I jumped up from my desk, throwing my homework aside. He was holding a box. I peeked inside.

"Is it a monkey?" I asked. Daddy laughed.

"It's a Siamese kitten," he snickered. "All ten-year-old girls need a kitten to love."

I had always been a cat lover. A car had hit my cat a few weeks earlier. My Daddy found him, but didn't tell me. Every morning and every night, for several weeks, I searched diligently for my calico cat and best friend. Daddy immediately began looking for the perfect replacement. It broke his heart to hear my desperate cry for my lost friend.

He could have looked the world over, but wouldn't have found a better friend than Messee. She was nothing but a tiny bundle of fur the day that she joined our family. I carefully lifted her out of the box, but she ran and hid in my closet. Finally, a few hours later, she ventured out, crawled into my lap and began purring. She found a new home in my lap. From that day forward, Messee was my companion. She slept with me every night. When I went outside to play, Messee went along with me. She stayed as close to me as possible.

One day several years later, we discovered that Messee would soon become a mother. We found her a comfortable box, put soft towels in it and encouraged her to use it, as her due date was drawing near. She didn't like the box idea, however. She wanted to sleep with me. We had always been bed partners and as far as she was concerned, we would continue to sleep together, regardless of her approaching arrival.

One night, after everyone in the house was fast asleep, I turned over in my bed and heard a tiny "mew." My bed had become a maternity ward. "Mom!" I shouted. "Please come in here." Since the lights were out, I was afraid to move in the dark, for fear of rolling over on one of the newborn kittens.

We were surprised when the lights came on. We saw five tiny babies in the bed with Messee and me. My mother picked them up, placed them in the box and changed my bed linens while I took a shower. Finally we all went back to sleep. The next morning when I awoke, Messee and her five babies were sleeping right by my side. The seven of us shared the bed together each night for the next six weeks. We didn't start out sleeping together, but as soon as the house got quiet, Messee carried her babies, one-by-one, back to my bed with her.

When I stretched out on the couch to watch television after dinner, Messee and her five kittens joined me. Messee loved me dearly, but she loved her kittens too! Her solution was simple: they all sat in my lap.

Eventually the kittens grew up and found homes away from home. My lap grew emptier and emptier until finally Messee curled up in my lap alone again. We missed her babies, but we still had each other.

The day that I moved out, quite a few years later, I was sad to leave Messee behind. At her age, Messee would have had a difficult time adjusting to a new environment, so I left her in my mother's care.

Years later, after my twin sons were born, we spent the first two weeks with my parents. I'll never forget the day that I arrived from the hospital with my newborn sons. I sat down on the couch with a baby in each arm. Suddenly, Messee jumped in the middle of my lap. She looked at each baby and then up at me. She began to purr. She was very proud of my tiny babies, just as I had been proud of hers.

"We did it again didn't we, Messee?" I whispered into her ear. She curled up in my lap and fell asleep. During the time we were there, when I sat down with a baby, I held a cat too! It brought back memories from many years earlier when I held Messee and a lapful of kittens. Both Messee and I loved each other dearly, but we also loved our babies too! Again, the solution was simple. After my babies were born, they and Messee sat in my lap. As my twins grew bigger, the three of them became quite a lapful of love.

A Purrfect Pet Project

ROBERTA SANDLER

$\mathcal{L}$ittle cats have radar. They know exactly where to find my daughter, and once they find her, I suspect they scatter some kind of "sympathy dust" around her.

What I couldn't figure out was whether these cute, stray balls of fur actually tagged along behind her, or whether she picked them up and carried them home. Most times, I told her, "No," and that was the end of it. But Jodi was clever. One day she came home after school with her fifth-grade teacher to back her up.

"This helpless kitten followed Jodi to school today, so the students and I made a little box for it out of newspapers and cardboard," Mrs. Palladino explained to me. "Will you permit Jodi to keep the kitten? It seems to have become attached to her."

Oh, great. I wasn't especially crazy about cats. I'm more of a "dog" person. Clever Mrs. Palladino, a partner in crime with my daughter, had even picked up a box of cat food so that we could feed the animal. As unenthusiastic as I felt about this, I couldn't bring myself to say no to my child's teacher. Before I could reply, Jodi pleaded with me. "Mom, this kitten is an orphan. He needs me. I promise I'll take care of him."

That's how Pepper insinuated himself upon our household. I gave my approval, on condition that Jodi keep him in the garage and not inside the house. Mrs. Palladino smiled and said goodbye. She turned to wink at Jodi as she walked from our driveway back to her car.

Jodi carried the kitten gingerly to the garage and laid out an old beach towel for the feline to sleep on. I brought a small bowl of water to Pepper, the name Jodi had bestowed upon the animal. Pepper was black and white, with tiny white boots for paws. I began sneezing. My eyes felt watery. Uh-oh!

Within a few weeks, Pepper had moved into Jodi's bedroom, and I bravely ignored my sneezing. My daughter was devoted to her little buddy, and he made himself comfortable by sleeping in her bed with her. When Jodi was at school, I popped allergy pills, and became pals with Pepper, whose affection melted my heart.

"He looks so cold and hungry," Jodi exclaimed about six months later, as she pointed to a tiny gray kitten perched on our doorstep. The miniscule animal shivered and cried. Only a heartless soul could turn him away.

"Oh, all right," I acquiesced. "You can keep him in the garage until morning, but then you'll have to let him loose."

At 3 a.m., I wearily went down to the garage. I couldn't sleep. I tried counting sheep, but all I could imagine were helpless little kittens trying to jump over a fence. The tiny being hurried over to purr at my feet. I shouldn't have come down to visit him. I shouldn't have petted him. And I certainly shouldn't have picked him up. That night, the gray angora kitten moved into our kitchen. Jodi named the kitten Sniffles, in honor of me. When we turned him over, we discovered that he was a she. And she was adorable.

"Mommy, isn't he cute?" Jodi asked me several weeks

later, as she held in her arms a small striped kitten. I sighed.

"Okay, Jodi, where did this one come from?" Jodi put the cat down and he ran between my feet and parked himself there.

"My friend Rochelle's cat just had a litter, and her mother doesn't want six kittens, so I said we'd adopt one. Please, please, Mom? We'll keep him in the garage."

I shook my head. "Oh, no. Twice I've been suckered in by that ploy. I'm not running a harem for homeless cats." The brooding expression on Jodi's face was more than I could bear. The kitten, now named Tiger, spent the night in the garage. I warned Jodi that in the morning I intended to let Tiger loose, and if he came back, he could stay with us, and if he didn't come back, we'd chalk it up to wanderlust and ingratitude.

Tiger refused to budge when I raised the garage door in the morning. I walked outside to the curb and beckoned, "Here, kitty, kitty." Tiger remained glued to the beach blanket.

Two cats were enough. I absolutely would not have three cats in my house. I told that to Tiger as I drove him to the town marina, where fishing boats were docked.

"Can you smell all that fish?" I asked Tiger. "Yummy. Doesn't it smell good?" Tiger stared at me with his poker face as he sat curled up in the passenger seat. He wasn't making this easy for me.

"Tiger, you'll never go hungry," I told him. "That fish is your daily din-din. It's a cat's paradise, here. Out of the car!" I swung open the passenger door. Tiger uttered a pitiful little meow.

"Don't flash those baby blues at me," I firmly said. "You know what I'm saying. Now go."

I reached for the kitten. He climbed into my arms and licked my face, his tiny body vibrating with soft, purring sounds. If only he hadn't thrown me that irresistible expression of trust and confidence. If only he didn't look so vulnerable. I probably would never have driven him back home, opened the front door, and let him gleefully step inside. Just what I needed. Tripli-cats.

Jodi was ecstatic when she came home from school and found three playful cats waiting for her. "You see, Mom," she said, pointing to the supermarket shopping bag that Tiger had climbed into, and was "walking" across the kitchen floor. "Tiger likes it here."

I sneezed, rolled my eyes heavenward, and sighed. "I know, Jodi. I know."

The Cuckoo

VICTORIA RIES

While I was growing up in England in the early sixties, I loved going for long walks up sunny, country lanes. I enjoyed listening to the sound of the birds chirping and singing their happy songs, and to watch them swoop to catch a morsel to eat. As I walked along, the breeze would gently rustle the long grass by the roadside, and the dappled sunbeams would dance all over the damp, sandy lane. The trees were tall—oaks, birches, elms and sycamore. I realized then that Mother Nature was, indeed, a beautiful, powerful companion in my life.

It was on my way back from one of my many walks in the countryside that I heard a distress call coming from the deep, tangled undergrowth at the base of an enormous, majestic oak tree. On closer inspection, I found it to be a featherless baby bird, cold, hungry and frightened. I looked around to see if its mother was nearby, but there was no trace of her anywhere. I realized this fragile, naked baby bird would die if it wasn't warmed and fed immediately.

Gently I picked the tiny creature up, along with some dry grass it had fallen into, and placed it carefully inside my warm jacket. I could feel the little bird trembling during the quarter-mile walk home, but he was warming up and was quite cozy by the time I reached my house.

My mother wasn't too encouraging, and told me the baby bird would probably die during the night, without his mother to take care of him. We placed him in a small cardboard shoebox, with plenty of cotton balls surrounding him.

I warmed up a little milk and carefully fed the helpless bird with an eyedropper. I gently put him back in his comfy, warm shoebox, and hoped he'd make it through to the next feeding time.

I fed him every two hours, without fail. Miraculously the little bird survived the night. I ran to my mother and was hardly able to contain myself as I excitedly told her about the bird. She was extremely surprised!

The baby bird continued to feed and grow rapidly. He had head feathers now, and was looking plump and healthy. He began to know when I was around, and chirped merrily when he heard me coming. He thought I was his mother! I was flattered, of course, and felt pleased that he looked on me as his Mum!

Every day he grew larger and larger, and as he got his permanent feathers, I realized by his markings that he was a cuckoo! He'd progressed to a diet of chopped-up worms, and guzzled them ravenously. I loved him dearly.

One day, I went into the shed, and to my amazement he was flying! All around the room, he flew—looking for a way to freedom. I realized it would be cruel to keep him cooped up in the shed when he wanted so desperately to soar above the treetops with the other birds. I told my mother what had happened, and she suggested I take him back to where I found him, then let him go free.

Sadly, I caught him and put him in a large cardboard box. I carried him in front of me, as I trudged the quarter mile to where I'd found him. Tears streamed down my cheeks as I opened the box and gently uttered my good-byes, in between sobs of sadness. He hesitated for a moment—then looked around him, and with an almighty flapping of wings, he flew up, up into the sky and perched on a branch overhead. I looked up at him, and knew he was where he belonged, wild and free.

The Old Red Barn

MARY M. ALWARD

Thoughts of childhood days on the farm in rural, southern Ontario often come to mind.

On a cold winter's day, I would push open the wooden door of the old, red barn and bask in the coziness of its dim interior. Pungent smells greeted me. As I made my way down the aisle, I would stop every few stalls and greet my animal friends.

The black and white Holstein cows stood, twenty-eight in number, along the corridor. Some were ornery creatures, some meek and mild. Much like humans, each had her own distinct personality and each had been given a name. I can't recall all of their names. Grandpa bought and sold cows frequently. But there are a special few that remain as vivid in my mind today as they were forty years ago.

My favorite was Betty, the best milk producer of the dairy herd. Like most cows, she had big brown eyes and long lashes. She had distinctive black markings on a white background— unusual markings in large splotches down her sides and rump. On her forehead, was a large black spot with a white star in the center.

Whenever I entered the barn, Betty would give a low moo, as if saying hello. As I approached, she'd turn her head, watching my every move. I would step in beside her and scratch her forelock. She would close her eyes and rub against me; delighted someone was giving her attention.

Behind the cow stalls, old Oscar, the Holstein bull, stood next to the window to the horse barn. Now Oscar could be an ornery and temperamental creature, but he had a soft spot for this wee girl. Often, I would go into the horse barn and let myself into Oscar's stall. He would turn his head, blow through his nose and snort. He never moved. This was somewhat miraculous as when the men tried to move him he would snort, kick and shake his head angrily. I have seen him lift my uncle off his feet while trying to lead Oscar to the creek for water. Today I look back on my foolishness and wonder why I wasn't killed. Possibly Oscar understood that I was only a child. Or possibly there was a soft side to his nature not understood by adults.

The calf pen was always a delight to visit. I loved to pet the calves and take them their daily pail of milk after they were weaned. They would suck the milk through their noses, and when finished, butt the pail urging it to produce more, just as they had their mothers while they were suckling. One day, a calf pulled the pail from my hands, pushed her head into it, and it became stuck, the bail clinging to her ears. I chuckle remembering the time I had retrieving that pail.

At the back of the barn was the pigpen. Usually there were three to four sows housed here. One of my favorite things was watching the mother pig suckling somewhere from eight to ten piglets. She'd lie on her side, eyes closed, while her babies squealed and fought over a teat.

The only thing I didn't like about the barn was the silo. Each fall, the corn was harvested, put through the corn chopper and blown into the forty-foot silo. This would provide ensilage for the cattle during the harsh Ontario winter.

One cool November day, my uncle asked me to go up into the silo and throw down the ensilage. I agreed. When the task was completed, I stepped to the entrance to descend the ladder. As I looked out, the ground swirled. Fear slithered along my spine. I stood, paralyzed. There was no way I could get down. I waited, rather impatiently, until my uncle came to my rescue. I never entered that silo again.

The haymow was one of my favorite places. When I was very young, the hay was cut, thrown onto a wagon with racks, taken to the barn and pitched into the upper level of the barn by hand. In later years, it was baled. I remember helping stack the bales in the mow. Even today, the fragrance of freshly mown hay carries me back over the years to the haymow of the old, red barn where mice played and barn owls pounced on their prey.

The straw stack behind the barn was a delight to us children. When playing hide-and-go-seek, we would wiggle into the prickly straw and cover ourselves. This was the best hiding place of all. When found, we would emerge, straw clinging to our clothes and hair. If Grandpa found us burrowing into the straw stack, we would get a sound scolding. This never stopped us from returning to our refuge time after time.

One memory that I look back on with fondness involved my favorite cow, Betty. It was a dark, rainy day. When I entered the barn, instead of the usual low, gentle moo, I heard Betty bawling ferociously. I approached slowly, wondering what on earth could be wrong. One glance told me that Betty was in trouble. She was in hard labor and her calf was arriving in a breech position.

I burst through the door of the house and in short, panting gasps told my uncle what was happening. We hurried to the barn and with some hard work, shared by human and animal, a healthy young heifer was born.

That was my first glimpse of the birthing process. What a thrill to watch a new life enter the world! The calf stood on shaky legs. Betty heaved to her feet and coaxed the calf to suckle. An awesome experience for a small girl of ten.

Recently, I took a drive to the rural community where I grew up. I stopped my car on the gravel road and sat, looking at that old, red barn. Yes, it's still standing, though the red paint has faded and it is somewhat in disrepair. But for a few moments, the sounds and smells of that cozy structure whirled through my mind. I will never forget the good times I spent in that old, red barn.

Quacky

THELMA TAYLOR

Quacky came into our lives as an Easter duck. I was never too fond of the idea of giving ducks for Easter because I'm sure some are abused and neglected when many of the kids who receive them as gifts consider them toys rather than living creatures to nourish and respond to.

When my kids were three and four, they had to have baby ducks and they got them through some source. The ducks were with them every minute of their waking hours. The ducks quacked loud and long when they were separated from the kids.

Naptime was the most distracting. Ours was a long, old, stone farmhouse that was very soundproof. The kids would wait until I got busy, sneak out of bed, get the ducks and put them under the covers with them. The ducks never made a quack, but when I went to check on the kids, I'd find the ducks had poked their heads from under the covers and had their long necks and bills lying flat on the pillow next to each child.

The kids would hurry outside with the ducks as soon as they woke up. They were automatically potty trained. There was never a mishap. When I checked on the sleeping foursome, I pulled the ducks from their resting place and plopped them in their pens. They let me know they were displeased with the arrangement.

I kept telling the kids, "One day you'll forget and the ducks will jump off the bed and break a leg." They assured me that they would never forget. They did and I did. Then Quacky jumped and broke a leg. Nobody said anything. I didn't even say, "I told you so" because the results of their misbehavior was evident every day.

Quacky lived the length of two duck life spans and remained faithful to the kids. Wherever they went, he was sure to follow, quacking in a contented monotone. My son David made pets of all farm animals that would comply, and they followed him. He fed the animals in the mornings. There were three barns and he made a triangular path that took him across the carport. The Border collie was always ahead of the line. He had to show them all that he knew the road. Sometimes the pony would vie for first place in the parade and there'd be a squabble. Pet lambs didn't care. The pet pig was always huffing and grunting last in the line. Quacky stayed out from under their feet, but as close to David as he could safely get.

We got other ducks to be companions to Quacky. They would always get caught in the pond by turtles or by other predators, but Quacky escaped unharmed.

When migrating ducks came by, Quacky would look up and quack urgently to call them down. He succeeded time and again. They'd swim on the pond below the house with him and he'd be ecstatic. He'd quack to us and turn and quack to them. We assumed he was telling us that they were going to stay and telling them that our place was a wonderful home.

As the visiting ducks began to fly away, he started his sales pitch to get one or two to come to the house and live with him. He'd travel a short distance in front of the wild ducks and they would come closer and closer to the house. You could hear the excitement in his voice. Then a clump of them would go back to the pond and he'd go into his pleading dialogue.

There would always be one or two that would really consider giving up the wild life. They would get halfway between the house and the pond. When the last one turned around and hurried back, you could see depression descend on Quacky. He'd follow them back to the pond, never giving up until they all flew away. We would be so sad because we knew he'd build up hope for the next group and have to face loneliness again.

He lived a very lengthy life for a duck, and then one night he disappeared. We assume that in his old age he was not quick enough to escape a predator. We know he was wise enough, but probably not speedy enough.

Funeral Prayer

DEAN TOLMAN

Note from the submitter, Maureen Tolman Flannery:

When we were little girls on the sheep ranch, my sister and I were given orphan lambs to bottle feed and, by the end of the summer, they followed us around like the nursery rhyme. When two of our pet lambs died at the same time, it was a true family disaster complete with much weeping. We wrapped their bodies in blankets and carried them to the end of the horse pasture where my father had prepared a joint grave. He had written this poem which we continued to use, with only slight alteration, for the funerals of the many nursed and cared-for animals who needed funerals in the years to come. I then went on to use it for the internment of my children's pets and when we buried wild animals. My father is now 85 years old and continues to nurse every injured wild thing he encounters. Here is the prayer he wrote for his little girls' (about four and six years old) first personal encounter with death.

𝓗ere lie two

little lambs of mine.

We lay them to rest

'neath the warm sunshine.

One was Dean,

and one Lulabelle.

They were good little lambs

and we loved them well.

But "from ashes to ashes,

from dust to dust,"

they were born into the world

and return they must.

So to heaven they go,

with all our love—

to romp and play

with God above.

from ANIMAL BLESSINGS

Loving Again

NANCY B. GIBBS

$\mathcal{E}$arly one morning Star had a litter of kittens. She faithfully brought kittens into this world on a regular basis, and since she normally had three or four at a time, we struggled to find good homes for them. Every once in a while, however, we kept one of her offspring. This particular time one of her babies was a gray tabby kitten with green eyes. Stripy had a wonderful personality. He was playful yet loving.

Brad and Chad, our twin sons, were about nine years old at the time Stripy was born. They adored him and decided right off that Stripy would be a keeper. Their cat friend loved them almost as much as they loved him. Stripy liked all of us, but he followed the boys everywhere they went.

Stripy had an older sister, Menos, who was born about six months earlier. As you can probably guess, Menos was a keeper, too! She was the spitting image of a Siamese kitten and reminded me of my childhood friend, Messee. Menos loved my daughter, Becky, so it all worked out well: the boy kitty loved the boys, the girl kitty loved the little girl. But when the house got quiet, Menos and Stripy loved each other. If the two of them were not playing together, they were wrapped up sleeping together somewhere in the house.

As the kids got older, of course, the cats did, too. Stripy's and Menos' playtime was converted into long naps together. When I was at home alone, they ignored me. When the kids came home, however, the cats came alive. Stripy tussled with the boys, while Menos played the piano with their sister. While Becky practiced her music lessons, Menos walked up and down the keyboard. She was a very talented cat, and her rhythm was almost perfect. Unfortunately, when she decided to play the piano at three o'clock in the morning, it didn't amuse any of us, including Stripy.

For eleven long years, Stripy and Menos were members of our family. We made three moves with them, and as long as they had each other, they were happy no matter where we called home. They explored the new houses and before long, they behaved as if they were right at home. As they got older, the kids were busy with teenage responsibilities and didn't want to play as much, either. But when the boys returned home each night, one of the two of them ended up with a lapful of kitty. When Becky played the piano, Menos continued to make a joyful sound with her.

Too soon, Brad and Chad went off to college, leaving Stripy behind. Each time they came home, however, Stripy purred and ran to them. They held him for hours at a time and talked about how much they missed him. They lived over sixty miles away.

During one visit, Chad became very concerned. "Feel this knot on Stripy's neck," he whispered. "Would you please take him to the veterinarian tomorrow, Mama?"

"Sure, I will," I said. "Don't worry, Stripy will be fine."

The vet drained the cyst and we hoped for the best. Before long, however, Stripy began limping and the knot came back. Quickly, his leg became like gelatin. It was obvious that he was in pain.

How would I tell the boys if he has cancer? I worried. I took Stripy back to the veterinarian's office. Later that day, she called me with the grim news.

"Stripy is in severe pain," she confided. "The tests confirm that he has a fast-growing type of cancer. If we operate and take out the tumor—and if he lives—he will also have to have his leg amputated. The humane thing to do is to put him to sleep," she said, her voice faltering.

I broke down and cried. I hated losing Stripy, but I hated even more having to call my sons to give them the news. I decided to tell them the prognosis and let them decide what to do. I tried to talk without emotion or tears.

"We're on our way," Brad said. "Don't do anything until we get there."

When they arrived home, they were very upset. "We want to see Stripy one more time," Chad whispered. "We want to say goodbye." I knew the decision had been made on their way home.

Together, the five of us went to the veterinarian's office. As soon as we walked in, the aide took us to the back of the clinic. The veterinarian came in and immediately began to explain the diagnosis to Brad and Chad. With tears in their eyes, they both gave her permission to release Stripy from his suffering. The five of us stood crying while we said our final goodbyes to our long-time friend.

When we walked out into the waiting room, all the employees and clients were hanging their heads. To see two grown boys saying goodbye to their cat was not easy for any of them or for us.

None of us could stay while the injection was given, although we told the vet that we would be back for Stripy's body.

Quietly, we drove home. Nobody said a word. When we walked inside the house, everyone went in a different direction.

I decided to go back to get Stripy myself. I got in my car and started to back out of the driveway. Brad came running out the back door and motioned for me to stop.

"I'll go with you, Mama," he said. "You don't need to go alone."

When we returned home, Chad was helping his father dig a grave. Becky had made a cross out of two sticks. We had a proper funeral for Stripy, and when I looked back toward the house I saw Menos sitting on the back of the couch, looking out the window. In my heart, I knew that she was saying good-bye to Stripy, too.

Putting Stripy to sleep was one of the hardest things our family has ever had to do. Before long, however, we could talk about him without tears. Our fond memories of him have lasted all these years.

This past January, Brad called home. "Do you know what today is, Mama?" he asked.

"No, I don't," I replied. "What?"

"Six years ago today, Stripy died. I still miss him," he whispered. "That was one of the saddest days of my life." I thought back to that day and tears filled my eyes.

A week ago, Brad called me. "Guess what, Mama!" he shouted. "I've got a new kitty. He is so cute. He acts as if he loves me just as much as Stripy did."

Losing a pet is never easy, no matter what our age. In my heart, I know that the best way to heal a hurt is to risk loving again. Brad had to make that decision for himself. Now I'm convinced that Rummy, his new kitten, has filled the empty spot that Stripy left in Brad's heart.

A few nights ago, my telephone rang. "Rummy's sad, Mama," Brad said, laughing.

"Why?" I chuckled.

"He hasn't met his new grandmother yet."

This weekend I'm going to meet the fuzzy little rascal who mended my son's broken heart.

Three Little Fish

CHERYL MORIKAWA

Who would have thought, three fish in a bowl
Could teach so many of life's lessons
To a four-year-old.

Lessons of love, caring for another
Lessons of responsibility,
Of being their "mother."

Lessons of loss, that life does end
Lessons of heartache,
Of missing a friend.

Lessons of faith, of unending love
Lessons of trust
In Heaven above.

Three little fish, how did God know
Would teach so much
To a four-year-old.

from ANIMAL BLESSINGS

Sammy

KEVIN GLAESMAN

The tired school bus crept along at about the same pace as my four-year-old brother eats his oatmeal. Sliding down and propping my knees up on back of the seat in front of me, I went over the plan for the afternoon. Sammy and I had recently found an old sluice box on one of the creeks up the valley behind our place. I knew, with a little digging, there was a fortune in gold awaiting us and I was anxious to get started. As we tediously wound our way along the narrow ribbon of highway, I daydreamed about the way Sammy and I met.

Sad brown eyes peered out at me from the corner of his cage. Some kind of Labrador retriever mix, I guessed. Cautiously, he padded over and took a tentative sniff of my hand through the wire mesh. Sitting back on his haunches, he cocked his head and looked up at me, as if to say, "Are you going to get me out of this madhouse, or what?"

Madhouse was right. The noise was deafening. Every kind of canine known to man barking and yelping at the top of their lungs. At the end of the walkway bordered by cages stood a rusted iron door. I knew what lay behind it. Sammy was on death row. Any second I expected one of the guards to come in and select an unfortunate for gassing. I imagined the hush that would fall over the crowd as the victim was dragged, paws scrambling for purchase, to his fate. The heavy iron door slamming shut with finality and then shortly a hideous hissing sound. The second it stopped, the uproar began again in earnest. "Help!!! Get us out of here!!!!"

I looked back down at Sammy. Funny, I already had him named. Tail wagging furiously, he quivered with anticipation. He knew. Fifteen minutes later, and with my dad twenty dollars lighter, I led him on a short leash out to our old station wagon.

I needed Sammy as much as he needed me. Shy, skinny and gawky, I had few friends and our isolated home made it difficult to mix with other kids.

My parents had acquired land, which in the early 1900's supported a small mining community served by the Alaska Railroad. Although now abandoned, the wooded hills around our house were dotted with small cabins and old mining camps which provided an endless supply of adventures. Sammy loved to take the lead and scare up rabbits. He never tired of running them down even though I never saw him hurt one. It was a great game to him. After finally cornering the hapless victim, he would bark at it a couple of times, just to let it know he had won. Then he would lope up to me, covered with sweat and bits of grass, grinning like he was going to be on the cover of *Field & Stream*.

Could this bus possibly move any slower? What if claim jumpers were eyeing the old sluice box? Fidgeting in my seat I thought back over our summer together.

We had climbed a mountain behind our place and claimed its rugged peak. We drove off a hoard of barbarians who were threatening our valley. We even rescued a helpless maiden from a vile dungeon. (OK, the barbarians were a busload of tourists who stopped to take pictures in front of our house, and the maiden was my sister, whom we let out of the outhouse after my brother nailed the door shut.) Sammy was my best friend. He was always glad to see me and he never made fun of me or picked on me. With Sammy by my side our days were filled with exploring and mischief, and I hated it when our escapades were cut short by something as mundane as bedtime.

Our nightly ritual seldom varied. I would crawl into bed and then Sammy would lick my face before settling down on the floor next to my bed. Sometimes, if I didn't think my parents would check in on me, I would let him lie down on the bed with me. Lying there, facing each other, we would play the eye game. I'd close my eyes and wait for a few seconds and then open them, and if his eyes were closed I'd stare at him. If he started to open his eyes I'd close mine real quick. I'm not sure what the object of this game was, but it usually ended up with us wrestling on the bed until my dad's voice reverberated from the hallway.

"Get that dog out of your bed and go to sleep!"

FINALLY the bus lurched around the last curve and shuddered to a halt in front of the hill up to our house.

I sensed something was wrong as soon as the bus deposited me on the highway shoulder. No black blur streaking down the hill to greet me. Racing up to the house I checked my room and asked Mom if she'd seen Sammy.

"Not for a while," she said. "He's probably out back."

Exiting through the back door I headed up the hill behind our house. He could be anywhere. The woods stretched out endlessly. Maybe he had gotten into trouble with a bear or coyote. We had both in abundance around our house. I began to make the rounds of the places we had explored together. My calls echoed off the hills and trailed off into the distance. As I eliminated one possible place after another I began to feel a deep foreboding. It began to get dark and as I made my way back down to the house I could just make out the narrow highway below our property. That possibility was too horrible to consider. I tried to push it out of my mind. Sammy never went down there without me. He got a whack for even looking like he might go down there.

Reaching the house, I made one more quick check. No Sammy. My stomach tightened as I realized I was going to have to check the road. Grabbing a flashlight I headed down the driveway.

In the gloom it was difficult to see. The feeble rays from my flashlight were almost instantly swallowed by the dark. I picked my way along the shoulder of the road carefully. The edge gave way to a steep bank which dropped about forty feet to the mud flats below.

The whine was faint but unmistakable. Sammy. Shining the light down over the bank I could just make him out, lying in the mud. Scrambling down the bank, I set the light so I could check him. He was hurt bad. He couldn't lift his head but he stopped whining as I gently rubbed his forehead. Realizing I had to get help, I told him to hang on and flew up to the house.

Choking back tears, I told my dad what had happened. He grabbed an old shed door and followed me down to Sammy. Laying the door flat, he slid him as gently as he could onto it. Hoisting the ends we cautiously began to make our way back up to the house.

We laid Sammy down next to my bed and Dad began to explain the situation to me. His back was broken. Even if it would help, which it wouldn't, there wasn't a veterinarian available. Sammy was not going to live, and the sooner he was put out of his misery the better. I couldn't bear it. My selfish fear of losing him won out over his well-being. I pleaded with Dad to leave him with me through the night. Sammy was lying quietly for the moment, and seeing this my dad finally relented. After covering him up to his neck with a blanket, I lay down on the edge of the bed, and while stroking his ears I prayed with all the earnestness an eleven-year-old boy contains.

"Please, God," I prayed, "let Sammy be OK."

After a while I drifted into a fitful sleep.

A cold nose pressed into my face, followed by a wet lick. Sammy! Astonished, I sat up and saw that Sammy had climbed into bed and laid down with his face next to mine. He whined softly. Scratching the back of an ear, I laid my cheek on his shoulder and listened for his heartbeat. Very faintly, through his thick coat, I could hear a humming sound. It stopped and I knew Sammy was gone. Burying my face in his fur I cried myself to sleep.

The next morning Dad and I buried Sammy in a grassy meadow behind our house.

I learned a lot from Sammy during our short time together. He gave me true friendship with unconditional love, and in the end he taught me lessons of loss and grief. Perhaps the greatest gift he gave was when he crawled into bed to lick me one last time. So a young boy would know his prayer had been answered and he was OK.

Security

JESSIE EYER, age 11

The house is brightly lit,
but yet something is still missing.
The cheery noises of the house,
the clattering of dishes.
A cold, blank feeling jolts your stomach,
as the door to your room slowly starts to open,
But it is only the cat.
The soft, thick, velvet warm fur,
the low, smooth, thick, silky purr
and those clever blue eyes
watching over you,
nuzzling its wet nose against you,
as you hold it in your arms.
A warm, soft feeling
comes into your stomach,
leaving the cold one to the never-ending night,
and know that everything will be all right.

from ANIMAL STORIES BY YOUNG WRITERS

DEVOTED COMPANIONS

"Perhaps we live together and are more fully contented, when we appreciate each other and take less for granted."

THOMAS L. REID

*A*nimals are such good listeners. You can tell them your secrets, your hopes, and certainly all your worries, and they never make you feel silly or insignificant. This is especially important when you're a child, when everyone else seems wiser and more capable than you are—and they let you know it. Everyone, that is, except the animals. They let you know that you matter.

Sweetie Pie

NANCY B. GIBBS

$\mathcal{I}$t seemed as if it had been just a few years since my home was filled with laughter and enthusiasm. Sometimes I longed for a few minutes of solitude and quiet, but most of the time I joined in the excitement. My children and I played with the pets and watched television together. Now I look back and realize that those were some of the most wonderful days of my life.

The years slipped by quickly, and the course of my life changed drastically. My twin sons grew up and moved away from home, and then a few years later my daughter followed them. She wasn't thrilled about going away to college, however.

"Why do things have to change, Mama?" she asked me one day, while she clung to our toy poodle, Daisey. There was no doubt in my mind that she didn't want to leave her beloved pets, but her apartment lease had made it perfectly clear: dogs and cats were strictly forbidden.

Becky had never lived without a pet to cuddle. I was afraid that she wouldn't be happy. During the week she attended the university three hours away, but each weekend she came home for a visit. We were always delighted to see her. She hated to go back to the apartment, leaving the pets behind, at the conclusion of each weekend.

After that lonesome year, Becky decided to move back home and commute to another college. The seventy-mile drive each day got very long, and after a few months she gave up on that idea, too.

Like many young people, she decided that she would join the workforce. I was pleased that she continued to attend extension classes, which were offered at the local high school. In my heart, however, I knew she wanted to attend college on a full-time basis. She simply couldn't part with her four-legged friends.

Before long, I was forced to face the dilemma of her moving out again when she landed a full-time job. Becky was in search of her independence, but this time she would be living only a few miles away from us.

Becky had been in her new home for only a couple of weeks when my telephone rang. "Will you please come over, Mama?" she begged. "I've got something I want to show you."

"Sure," I replied. "I'll be there in just a minute." I hopped into the car and went to her house. She met me at the door, holding a tiny black-and-white kitten. "Meet Sweetie Pie, Mama," she shouted gleefully. "I bought her at the pet store."

"Sweetie Pie is precious, Becky," I said, "but what about college? I was hoping that one day you would go back. You know how apartment managers can be about pets."

"I'll go back one day," Becky replied, "but Sweetie Pie will go with me the next time."

Just as I expected, a few months later Becky announced that she wanted to move again and further her education. This time, I was determined that Sweetie Pie would go along, if we had to check out every apartment in town.

The first apartment we looked at was perfect. And, to make

it even better, Becky's new landlady was kind enough to let Sweetie Pie live with Becky. We rejoiced as we signed the lease. Becky has been living in that apartment for over a year now, and she seems perfectly content with Sweetie Pie as her companion.

Once Becky had this black-and-white bundle of fur to love on a daily basis, she was able to get her priorities in order and had the desire to complete her college education. She followed her dreams, while Sweetie Pie kept her company.

Today, Becky is doing very well in college and is working on a double major. She seems to be happy and determined to obtain her degree. Somehow, in the back of my mind, I know that Sweetie Pie made all the difference. When pets have always been such an important part of a person's life, it's hard to live without them.

I'm so glad that Becky found a friend whom she could count on, for what should be some of the most wonderful days of her life—her college days.

My Friend Bob

DIANE M. CIARLONI

I was short. He was tall.

I was white. He was black.

My vocabulary was above average for a third-grader.

He . . . well . . . I was the only one who understood him when he "spoke."

I was a nine-year-old girl.

He was a beautiful, gorgeous six-year-old Tennessee Walking horse, and his registered name was Bob's Merry Legs. He was the most velvety black I'd ever seen. His four white stockings and broad white blaze made him look even blacker than he was. He was at least 16 hands high, which meant he towered over me. As I grew older, I realized the Tennessee Walking Horse Association should never have accepted him for registration since his left eye was that deep, dark brown most commonly associated with horses while his right eye was blue—commonly referred to as a glass eye.

I was nine and I thought his eye was beautiful. It simply added to the unique, magical qualities I already knew he possessed. I wanted him as soon as I saw him go into the sale ring. Daddy had brought me to the auction, but I'm sure he had no idea what would happen.

I couldn't take my eyes off the glorious-looking creature.

I was quite certain my life would be nothing but pure happiness if I could have him and, by contrast, I was equally certain it would be nothing but misery if I were denied.

I knew begging and pleading would get me nowhere. In our family, one made a simple request and then waited for the parental decision.

"How will you take care of him?" asked Daddy. "Look at him. He's huge. You won't even be able to get on his back."

I shook my head in the negative. "Yes, I will," I countered. "Before they took him into the ring I saw him stretch out with his front and back legs. I promise, Daddy, his belly was almost on the ground. I could have gotten on his back with no help."

"They want $125 for him," continued Daddy. "That's a lot of money, but that's not all. We'll need to feed him and pay for visits from the vet every now and then. We're talking about a very expensive situation here."

I looked him square in the face, eyeball-to-eyeball. "I could give you my entire allowance until he's paid off." Looking backward over all those years, I have no idea how Daddy kept a straight face.

"And how much allowance do you get?" he asked.

"A quarter every week."

"Hmmm," he said, "if my mental arithmetic is correct, you'll need almost 14 years to pay him off. That's a long time."

I dropped my head and looked down at the dirt. My visions of having the beautiful, black horse in the pasture at our small farm were fading quickly. Now my focus was to keep my bottom lip from quivering.

"Here." I looked up to see Daddy holding out a dime to me. I took it with a questioning look.

"Call your Mama and see how she feels about it." He

nodded toward the pay phone hanging on the wall of the sale barn.

I went to the phone and dialed the number. She answered almost immediately.

"Mama?"

"Is something wrong?" she asked before I could say anything else.

"No, m'am. Daddy wanted me to call you."

"Why?"

"Well, there's the most beautiful horse here. He's black and his name is Bob, and if you let me have him I'll give you my allowance to pay for him."

"Let me speak to Daddy."

I handed him the phone. He took it and turned his back, shielding his words from me. I waited. He finally hung up the receiver and rotated his body to face me.

"Are you sure about this? A horse is a lot of responsibility, you know. It's different from a dog or a cat."

I shook my head in the affirmative.

"Okay," said Daddy. "Go over to the man in the red plaid shirt, the one leaning against the fence. Ask him if the horse is still for sale for $125, and ask him if he can deliver him to our farm."

I couldn't believe it! I'd never before in my entire life experienced the surge of joy that rippled through me at those words. And, really, I'm sure I've never experienced it since then.

A grin split my face, so wide I could actually feel the shape of my cheeks changing. I ran to the man, began talking to him, pointing first at Bob and then at Daddy. He nodded his head "yes" to both my questions. I couldn't believe what was happening. I started to run back to Daddy but changed my mind.

I knew he'd take care of the business part. What I needed to do was introduce myself to Bob.

The big, black horse had been moved to a small corral, standing there all alone. There was hay in the manger but he seemed disinterested. I climbed to the top rail of the fence, threw one leg over at a time and perched there.

Daddy glanced up and saw me. "Be careful," he shouted. "Don't you get hurt before we even get him home."

Even now, all these years later, I can remember twisting my torso so Daddy could see my huge grin. I waved my hand, indicating all was well. I turned back to the horse.

"Hey, Bob," I said. "You're beautiful. You don't know me yet but I already love you. We're going to have wonderful times together."

The horse tossed his head before walking to me. He stopped three feet short, stretching out his neck and flaring his nostrils in an attempt to pull my scent into his nose. Slowly, I held out my hand. It was turned palm upward, flat. I don't really know how I knew that I was supposed to do it that way. I just did.

Bob snuffled across my small palm. His warm breath was the most wonderful sensation I'd ever felt. And I knew—at that moment—we'd bonded. Nothing else was needed. We were friends, and we would remain friends even after we died.

Bob settled in at the farm immediately. No fuss. No special fanfare. My parents did, however, set limits on the freedom we could enjoy. There was a railroad track one mile east of our house. I wasn't allowed to ride past it. There was a bridge ¾-mile to the west. I was allowed to ride *to* the bridge, but not on it or past it. There were numerous dirt roads crisscrossing our farm and I could ride anywhere I pleased on those.

We lived in the country and I attended private school in the city. I boarded a school bus at 6:30 in the morning and didn't return until 4:30. Bob learned my schedule. He began prancing and whinnying sometime between 4:05 and 4:15. Daddy made him wait until 4:20. Then he opened the paddock gate and let Bob walk, on his own with no bridle or rider, down the long driveway to the edge of the cattle gap. He waited there, looking expectantly in the direction he knew would bring the bus. He was neighing furiously by the time the bus door opened and I stepped out.

"Hi, boy," I'd greet him. "How were things for you today? Wanna' go for a ride?" And, of course, he always said yes.

My daddy always, always, always wore a hat; one of those dapper little fedora types. He would go nowhere without one perched on his head. At least, that was the case before Bob. There were, however, times *after* Bob when he had no choice.

Bob seemed to love those little hats. He waited for Daddy to walk past him and then, as quick as lightning, he darted over, snagged the hat with his teeth and snatched it from Daddy's head. He seemed to laugh and shout as he did it, knowing he'd exposed the very large bald spot. Fortunately, Daddy learned quickly that chasing the big, black horse was *not* the thing to do. It wasn't a fair match and Bob always won. Instead, just ignore the situation. Don't acknowledge the sight of Bob running around with the hat dangling from his big, yellow teeth. Eventually, having the fun taken from his game due to lack of attention, he would walk over and drop the hat at Daddy's feet.

Three years after Bob came to live with us, Mama and Daddy decided I could ride beyond the railroad tracks and beyond the bridge. That was really great but there was one major problem: I couldn't convince Bob we had permission to expand our universe. He absolutely refused to cross the tracks or the bridge. It was frustrating as well as humiliating. Finally, Daddy came and led him across both former boundaries while I sat in the saddle. Somehow, he equated that action with receiving the official okay from an authority figure.

I had my first date on Bob. His name was Malcolm— blond, braces on his teeth, skinny and beautiful blue eyes. I can't remember his horse but I do know he didn't begin to compare with Bob in either beauty or intelligence. We took a long ride together, Malcolm 15 and I 14. We took our tennis rackets and sandwiches Mama made. Bob kept watch as we munched and talked.

I graduated grade school (there was no such thing as junior high back then) and moved into high school. Unlike some girls, though, I didn't leave behind my passion for horses in general and for Bob in particular. He was still my very best friend, and he still met me each day at the end of the driveway. Very seldom did we skip a day of riding but, if we did, I sat in the pasture with him. Our conversations were long and slow and deep. There was nothing about me he didn't know, and he kept my secrets ever so well.

I was sixteen years old and completing my sophomore term. Bob had been my best friend for eight years but, in most ways, it seemed far longer than that. He, too, was 16 but his hair was still jet black and his step still had all the fire and prance of a much younger horse. I visited Bob each morning before walking down the driveway to meet the school bus, but there was something seriously wrong on this particular morning. He was on the ground in his paddock, drenched in sweat. He'd swing his beautiful head toward his side and try to nip himself, telling me he was experiencing painful stomach cramps. He looked at me. I knew he was asking for help, and I also knew he had a horrible case of colic.

Sometimes colic happens for no obvious reason. Somehow an impaction develops in the bowel. The pain is horrendous.

I ran to the house, slamming the door behind me, snatching the receiver from the wall phone and called the vet. Mama came from the kitchen, drying her hands on a dish towel.

"What's wrong?" she asked.

"It's Bob," I answered, short of breath from the run as well as fear. "Colic. I called the vet." I was struggling to hold back tears.

Mama walked to me and patted my shoulder. "It'll be okay," she said. "I'll just go get Daddy so he can help." She got into her car and drove to the field where he was working on his tractor. They returned together.

"We need to get him up if we can," he said to me. We set off for the paddock at a run. Daddy put a lead rope on Bob's halter. "You coax him," he said. "He'll listen to you."

I couldn't help it. I started crying. "Bob," I sobbed. "Please, Bob. Get up. Please. Please. I need you, Bob."

The big horse lumbered to his feet and, when he was standing, I gasped. He looked as if he'd lost 100 pounds over night. Daddy handed me the lead rope. "Walk him," he said tersely. I could tell from his look and his voice that he thought the situation was bleak. Tears running down my face, I started walking the black horse.

The vet arrived, jumping quickly out the door and pulling a stainless steel bucket from the back of his truck, pouring it half-full of mineral oil. He stuck a pump in the bucket with a long, clear plastic tube attached to it. He walked over to Bob, pinched his nostrils together and began feeding the tube through his nose, down his throat and into his stomach. I couldn't watch. It looked ghastly. He began pumping the oil into the tube, hoping to dislodge the impaction and move it out. He pumped and pumped and pumped, but nothing happened.

Bob's front legs started buckling at the knees.

"Don't let him go down," he yelled at me. "We don't want him to roll. If he does, he could twist that intestine and then we don't have a prayer."

I held on to him, my heart breaking. I knew he was miserable. I hated the tube. I knew how he must long to lie down. But I tugged and strained on the lead rope. "Please, Bob," I prayed. "Stand up, Bob." And, for the first time since the ordeal began, I allowed myself to say the word. The awful word. "Please, Bob. Please don't die," I breathed.

"I can't do anything more," the vet said. "Just keep walking him as much as you can." I was exhausted, but not too exhausted to continue helping the best friend I'd ever had.

I walked. I stroked his face. He touched my cheek with his nose. I suppose I knew what would happen. I suppose I wasn't surprised when he yanked the rope from my hand and crumpled to the ground, looking like a million broken pieces of black glass. He stretched out his neck, and I lay down on the grass next to him.

"I love you, Bob. You've been the best friend I could ever have." He knew what I said. He always did. I missed school for an entire week, crying every day.

I was still short. He was still tall.

I was still white. He was still black.

But the wonderful world of friendship erased every difference. And, all these many years later, my heart still feels the tug of a lead rope whenever I think of Bob.

Daddy is dead and Mama is more than 80 years old. The farm has long since been sold with rows of houses built on it. Way back in the corner . . . in the middle of a small thicket of trees and vines . . . is where Bob is buried. It was a big grave and Daddy worked all day to dig it. He knew a decent burial was all I'd accept for Bob.

There's a house built over the grave now. Sometimes, if I drive by there when I'm home visiting Mama, I wonder if the people living in that house ever hear a whinny and, just for a minute, think they've seen the silliest thing—a big, black horse with a fedora dangling between his teeth. I think they do. I think they see my friend, Bob.

From Terror to Trust

ED EAMES

My decision to train with a guide dog in 1981 came after months of weighing the pros and cons. I had spent the previous academic year in India pursuing research on the problems faced by government officers responsible for maintaining law and order in regions equivalent to counties in the United States. Most of my time was spent in Patna, the capitol of the state of Bihar, and, when not actively involved in collecting data, I spent most of my time self-confined in the apartment I was renting.

Just outside my door the streets were teeming with people and activities. However, as a newly-blind person, I felt particularly vulnerable when venturing forth alone employing the only mobility device I had been taught to use—a long white cane.

As soon as I left the house and entered the road (sidewalks did not exist in this area), I encountered crowds of people walking in all directions, meandering cows, water buffalo and other animals, buses and cars driven with one hand on the steering wheel and the other on the horn, bicycle rickshaws and bicycle riders shouting for the right of way, horse-drawn vehicles and every other imaginable form of transportation.

Trying to negotiate my way through this seemingly amorphous and uncontrolled mass of humanity, animals and traffic, I quickly gave up all attempts to go anywhere on my own.

Following my return to the United States, my experience in India, coupled with my need to travel from my home in Philadelphia to my job in New York, pushed me toward switching from a cane to a guide dog as my primary mobility aid.

My family and I did not think of ourselves as dog or pet people, so I had not previously considered getting a guide dog. Growing up during the depression in New York City, my family did not have pets. When I was in my teens, my brother Irv returned from Europe with two Boxers. His goal was to breed the pair and become one of the first to introduce New York City dog fanciers to the breed. During the several months he lived with my parents and me, my job was to watch over the dogs. I spent many an afternoon chasing one or the other of these two critters around the streets in the Bronx, which did not endear these masterful escape artists to me!

After my marriage and relocation to Philadelphia where I taught anthropology at Temple University, we remained petless for several years. However, as my two older children reached those dog-loving ages of five and six, we decided to adopt a collie mix from a friend who claimed she could no longer care for this marvelous canine companion. It quickly became apparent that Ginger had never been trained to do or obey anything, and on one of her many unauthorized excursions through the neighborhood got pregnant. Much to the dismay of my children, Mona and David, we gave the puppies away, and, shortly thereafter, passed poor Ginger onto some other unsuspecting friend. I frequently wonder what happened to her and if anyone with far greater knowledge than I possessed, was able to convert her into a member of the family.

One result of this unfortunate dog adoption was that my wife Phyllis became anti-dog. This feeling was something I would have to deal with many years later, if my transition from white cane to guide dog was to be successful. Although not overtly opposed to my decision, Phyllis could not hide her apprehension about sharing our house with a dog.

Following the trip to India, I went to The Seeing Eye in Morristown, New Jersey, where I met and welcomed into my life a black Labrador Retriever named Perrier. During our first few days together, I had to overcome some major problems. Although legally blind, I had some residual vision, and the first time Perrier opened his mouth I was appalled by his gleaming white teeth and the potential harm they could do to me, my children or grandchildren. However, during our four weeks of intensive training, I began to get an inkling of the capabilities of my new canine assistant and to depend more and more on his sight, training and intelligence to get around in environments totally new to me. These weeks served as an affirmation of my decision.

On returning home from guide dog school, I followed the advice of my trainer and kept visitors away to allow Perrier to get used to his new environment and continue the bonding process. In contrast to my 15-year-old daughter Lori's fondness for Perrier, as I expected, Phyllis was not overly thrilled with him joining the family. She accepted his presence because she saw him as a major force in maintaining my ability to commute between Philadelphia and New York City. She realized Perrier would be a great asset in helping me negotiate my way from Penn Station, where my commute ended, to my office at Baruch College in the heart of Manhattan.

When my daughter Mona visited with her children, Lauren and Rebecca, things did not go as smoothly as anticipated. One-year-old Rebecca, who was then crawling around, immediately bonded with Perrier and used him to help her stand as she began moving into the toddler stage. On his side, Perrier learned to sit under Rebecca's high chair in order to scarf any food she dropped on the floor. Rebecca soon caught on to this game, and would periodically drop chunks of food into his gaping mouth!

Three-and-a-half-year-old Lauren's reaction to my gentle 80-pound giant of a dog was very different. On their first meeting in my apartment, Lauren started screaming and shaking uncontrollably. Perrier, on leash for this introduction, had to be taken away and placed in another room. All of us tried talking to Lauren about what had frightened and upset her, but she was unwilling to talk about her fear. My daughter Mona called later that night to say Lauren was still upset and kept saying she did not want to go back to Grandpa's and Grandma's house.

The next time Lauren and Perrier met was in her house. We all felt she would be more comfortable in her own territory, and I kept Perrier on leash and near me during the entire visit. We tried to get Lauren to pet him, but she was having none of it.

Since daughter Mona, Lauren, Rebecca and son-in-law Arthur lived about half an hour drive away, Phyllis, Lori and I saw them at least once a week. Now these visits were being threatened by Lauren's obvious terror at Perrier's presence. Mona also indicated that whenever his name was raised, Lauren began crying or shaking.

It was obvious we all were going to have to work on this problem collectively and intensively. Perrier had become part of my life, and the thought of leaving him at home when we visited Mona and the family, or keeping him isolated in one of the other rooms while they visited us, was unacceptable.

For the next few months, I gradually brought Perrier into Lauren's presence by talking about him and having him join us for short intervals. As Lauren's fear began to abate, she was the one who asked to touch and pet him. Growing more and more relaxed, she asked me to remove Perrier's leash, but stay nearby. Now it was Perrier's turn to show he understood the situation.

Initially, sensing the fragility of the situation, Perrier did not approach Lauren and, when she approached him, he stood still, letting her make all the overtures. From petting him, she progressed to hugging, and in time tolerated his occasional quick lick.

At this point I introduced a new variable—Lauren was permitted to feed him. Before putting down the bowl with his dog food, I would put Perrier at a DOWN Stay where he would remain until given the signal to eat. Lauren was intrigued by this process, and initially asked if she could give him the signal. From there we progressed to her putting the bowl on the floor and then to having her help me in preparing Perrier's meal.

After several months of building the relationship between my granddaughter and my guide dog, I knew we had succeeded when I walked into our living room to discover Lauren was lying on the floor, watching television, with her head resting on Perrier's stomach! We had finally bridged the gap and Perrier was accepted as part of our family by everyone.

A Dog's Life

BEA SHEFTEL

$\mathscr{I}$ have had pets since I was a little girl. With me now are a black Tibetian terrier named Zima, and a blond Lab named Elmo. They are my daily companions and as close to me as children.

Every dog in my life has been special, but the first one remains a loving memory in my heart. Chrissy was a girl cocker spaniel who had been a Christmas gift to my cousins. They named her Christmas and then called her Chrissy for short.

My cousins and their two children lived in a second-floor, five-room apartment. As Chrissy grew from puppy to full size, they realized they couldn't keep her. She needed a place to run and they had no yard. So my cousins asked my mom if she knew of anyone who wanted to take Chrissy.

Mom worked full time. Even though her job was only a few blocks from home, she worried about us kids coming home to an empty house. I was eleven and in charge of watching my younger brother and sister after school. "A dog would be a good protection for my children," Mom said.

We lived in a one-family house with a big back yard. There would be no problem taking the dog for a walk since we could open a door and let her out. We set up a feed and walk plan so the burden of Chrissy's care wouldn't fall completely on my mother. Another cousin, Jim, also volunteered to help out. His mother wouldn't let him have a dog so he "adopted" Chrissy as his, too.

Now a cocker spaniel is not a watch dog, but Chrissy, even though a moderate-sized dog, was fiercely protective of us children. Before she came to live with us, the gas and electric companies insisted they had a right to access. This meant they'd go through our house to the basement to get to the yard. Since we kids were home alone for several hours after school, Mom was worried. Her calls to the utility companies to demand they restrict access to the hours when she was home were met with their claim of legal rights to access. This was back in the 1950's, and the laws were different. Today the utility companies will not enter a home unless an adult is present. Mom naturally was concerned about strange men wandering our home when we kids were home alone. So even though Dad wasn't so sure we should have a dog, Chrissy joined our family. Her bark was loud and threatening enough to keep anyone who didn't know how gentle she was from insisting on entering our home.

Chrissy followed us all over the house. When we kids played, she was right in the middle, joining in our games. She particularly loved running around the yard playing chase. A typical dog, she loved to run after a ball or play pull. It wasn't a few days before this black dog with the wavy hair won the hearts of everyone in the house, including Dad.

Money was tight, but Chrissy got the best dog food. Mom even heated it up for her. "Nobody likes cold food," she said.

Since both Mom and Dad worked, we kids were alone a lot, with too much time on our hands. We felt that scraps were a treat for Chrissy, so we gave her bits of our sandwiches. After dinner, we hid the remains in a bag to feed to Chrissy when our parents weren't around. Chrissy learned to love a variety of people food, from cookies to liverwurst.

Living in Brooklyn, New York, our lives had been severely restricted. While Mom was at work, we were forbidden to go outside except to sit on the stoop. With Chrissy as our dog companion, Mother gave us more freedom. Now, after school, we were allowed to go to the park. Chrissy loved the wide open spaces to chase after her ball (the kind that squeaked was her favorite). Every nice day we walked the five blocks to Winthrop Park. We played in a fenced-in area where our dog was safe from traffic.

I have had many dogs since Chrissy, but even though I loved them all, none was as well behaved as that little cocker spaniel. She learned quickly what was expected of her. There were no mistakes in the house, no chewed chair legs or crayons.

As our constant companion, Chrissy put up with our childish pranks. I remember one summer day we dressed her up in a hat, sunglasses and a scarf. She sat patiently while I photographed her with my Brownie camera. Only when we undressed her and said, "Good girl," did she jump off the chair.

She was a trustworthy dog. I mean, my Zima has jumped from the chair to the table to hunt for scraps. And Elmo can't be left alone in a room with food or he'll gobble it up (I found him one day with his head in the middle of a sheet cake, devouring the dessert). We had no fear of Chrissy ever doing anything like that. Usually. Well, sometimes temptation was too much and even Chrissy gave in to doggie hunger.

What happened was my fault. I thought it was cute to have Chrissy sit on a chair at the kitchen table while my brother, sister and I ate our lunch. We gave Chrissy a plate of treats so she could join us. Sometimes I made her a liverwurst sandwich, which was her favorite. She ate like a genteel lady, taking small bites of her food, without slobbering.

Saturday night was our family dinner night. Mom made a special dish such as a roast, or lasagna. This night we were having roast beef. Mom finished cooking it and put it on the kitchen table so the juices could settle. I was to set the dining room table. Mom brought in the iced-tea and poured it in the glasses. For some reason neither one of us realized Chrissy hadn't followed us as she usually did and was still in the kitchen.

The aroma of the roast filled the house and I could hardly wait to sit down to our favorite dinner. "Make the salad," Mom said.

I returned to the kitchen to prepare the salad when I screamed. Chrissy had the roast beef on the floor and was happily chomping on our dinner. Mom was furious, but not with the dog. It was I who was the recipient of her wrath. She knew I'd taught Chrissy how to jump on the kitchen chair. She'd seen us one day sitting at the table eating, with Chrissy next to us. "You are teaching the dog the wrong thing," she cautioned. "Dogs don't belong at the table."

That night I sat at the table and suffered the stares of my family. There was no meat for us. We had mashed potatoes, vegetables and salad for supper. Chrissy finished our roast, gave a loud burp and fell asleep on the living-room floor. After that, Mom put up a child safety gate to keep Chrissy out of the kitchen. She also had a talk with Chrissy. They say dogs don't understand, but I can truthfully say Chrissy never stole food from the table again.

On Christmas Eve my brother, sister and I wanted to buy our dog a new squeaky toy. We pooled our money and hoped we had enough. We went to the variety store near our house to pick out her present, and we saw several different sizes of snowmen squeaky toys. "We'll take the smallest one," I said, pointing to the toy.

"$1.50," the shopkeeper said.

I counted out our money. We were short about twenty-five cents. "We don't have enough. Can we owe you?" I asked. "It's a Christmas present for our dog." Another customer was selecting cards when he turned around.

"Go home and get the rest of the money," the shopkeeper insisted.

It was getting late. Soon the rest of the family would come over for our Christmas Eve gathering and we wouldn't be allowed back out. "Please," I begged, "I'll bring you the money after Christmas. This is for our dog. She's very special." There were tears in my eyes. My little brother and sister also sniffled.

The shopkeeper shook her head.

"We'll have to buy something cheaper," I said. But there was nothing. Defeated, we were about to leave when the other customer spoke up.

"Give the kids whichever toy they want for their dog. I'll pay," the kind-hearted man said.

"Thank you and Merry Christmas," we said as we skipped out of the store with our dog's present in a bag.

"Merry Christmas," the man called after us.

Christmas morning we all ran downstairs early, probably around 6 a.m. Chrissy was right with us. Before we headed for our gifts, we gave Chrissy hers. She ripped open the paper and tossed her new toy in the air. She ran after it, pounced on it, made it squeak, and tossed it in the air again. We laughed so hard we woke up our parents, and they came down to see which of our toys delighted us so much. They were surprised to see we hadn't opened our toys. The three of us were on the floor, playing with Chrissy.

Dad stood in the archway, his arms across his chest. "What's going on?"

"Look at Chrissy," I said.

The dog ran over to Dad with her new toy in her mouth. She dropped it at his feet. Smiling, Dad picked it up and tossed it and off she went again. Mom joined us and soon the whole family was playing with the dog. Mom and Dad also had special dog biscuit treats for Chrissy and a new bowl with her name on it. We didn't open our presents until much later. It was one of the best family Christmases. We learned a valuable lesson about the pleasure of giving instead of just receiving.

Chrissy gave us her unconditional love. She protected us kids from strangers with her bark, and also by putting her body in front of us when a stranger approached. She gave my mother a sense of security, knowing the dog was with us. And Chrissy loved each of us in a special way. When my little brother and sister frustrated me to tears and I ran off to cry in my room, Chrissy followed. She comforted me with her cold nose pressed against my face.

We spent many more Christmases with our wonderful dog. Our family went through many ups and downs. Dad lost his job. My parents feared they'd lose our house. My grandparents died. Through each event Chrissy was the one constant. Her love sustained us through the toughest times, and she always knew how to make us smile.

I was married the year Chrissy turned eighteen. She'd been through several operations to remove non-malignant tumors, but a few months later they would return. Mom came home from the last visit to the vet: "The doctor said he can't do anything more for Chrissy. If the tumors come back, she'll have to be put to sleep."

My brother, sister and I were adults. We knew that someday we'd lose our beloved dog, but nothing prepared us for the sad day when the tumors returned and Chrissy was in pain. It was time to let go of our canine companion who had become more than a dog to us. She was our babysitter, friend, confidant, and comforter. Dad went to get the car to drive her to her final visit to the vet.

"Say goodbye, now," Mom said. Chrissy sat on a plump pillow and was covered with a blanket. She looked at us with her big brown sad eyes.

"Are you sure the doctor can't help her?" I ran my hand over Chrissy's silky hair. "I don't want her to die."

"There's nothing more he can do. She's suffering," Mom explained.

My brother fought back tears. I couldn't help the tears which ran down my cheek. My sister hugged Chrissy and sobbed.

"Goodbye, Chrissy," I said, bending over to give our dog one last kiss. Her tongue came out to give me one last lick.

Dad drove Mom and Chrissy to the vet. Mom told us later, "I held her in my arms as the doctor gave her a shot. Her eyes closed, and it was as if she fell asleep on my shoulder."

No one could hold back the tears, not even my father and brother. Not even me now, more than 36 years after. She was a dog, but so much more. She was a part of our family, a dear member we loved as much as if she were another sister.

Mom and Dad are gone now too, and my brother, sister and I are all in our fifties, yet despite the decades which have passed we all have sweet memories of that dog who grew up with us. In fact, the snowman sits on a shelf in my brother's den, and Chrissy is enshrined in a frame in my house, a reminder of a special dog who gave us nothing but love.

When Barney Disobeyed

BYRON M.

$\mathcal{I}$ had always believed that Barney, our nine-year-old Saint Bernard, had been short-changed in the brains department. As a Canadian friend of mine used to say about dimwitted folks, Barney seemed a couple of sandwiches short of a picnic.

But my wife Iona and I loved the big brute, in spite of the fact that he was also clumsy and seemingly devoid of all approximations of graceful movement. If we bought a new lounge chair or a fragile lawn ornament, he would be certain to tip one over and break the other before the day was done.

And as a watchdog? Well, if a burglar broke into our place, Barney would probably hold the hoodlum's flashlight in his mouth to provide illumination while he rifled through our belongings.

We had talked about getting rid of Barney and acquiring a dog that would bark at intruders. Barney never barked at strangers, but he raised a ruckus each day when Karl, our mailman for the past ten years, pulled up alongside our mailbox.

"I think Barney believes it's rude to speak to strangers, so he only says 'hello' to the folks he knows and sees every day," Iona figured out one day as we pondered the mystery of why the big fellow only barked at people with whom he was acquainted.

But all the picky fault-finding aside, who was always there to listen to our troubles and to give us a sloppy kiss to cheer us up? Barney!

Who was always at our side when we went for nature walks, bravely keeping tigers and bears away? Why, Barney, of course.

And who was the first to greet us when we returned from work, and the last to say goodnight before we went to bed? None other than our good old buddy, Barney.

One lazy Sunday afternoon in late May, Iona and I were reading the paper when Barney suddenly roused himself from the nap he had been enjoying beside my easy chair. Emitting a strange, loud grunting sound that neither of us had ever heard before from the old boy, he got to his feet and began an urgent pacing that soon focused on the front door.

"He's ahead of schedule," Iona said, "but it's quite obvious that he needs to go out for a potty break."

I took that cool, clinical observation to be my cue that it was I who had been appointed to get up and let Barney out to obey the sudden call of nature.

Once he was in the yard, however, he gave no indication that he was in need of relieving himself. He howled—another thing neither of us had ever heard him do—then began to run swiftly down the gravel road that lay just beyond the small apple orchard at the rear of our property.

I called after him, commanding him to stop—and for the first time in his life, Barney disobeyed me.

Although we lived in a wooded area outside the city limits, the leash laws were very strict in our area. And since I had be- lieved I was only letting Barney out of the house for a quick comfort call, the big guy was devoid of leash and accompanying owner. As a responsible dog owner, I had no choice but to start down the road after him.

Barney ignored all my commands to return to me. He continued running until he ran around the bend forty yards ahead of me and disappeared from my sight.

As I trotted after him, realizing with each labored breath how woefully out of shape I had become, I worried that our beloved Saint Bernard had suffered some kind of mental breakdown.

Then, as I rounded the bend, I was horrified to see a late-model van that had apparently lost control on loose gravel and had skidded head-on into one of the massive oak trees that lined the road at that particular curve.

To my astonishment, I saw that our blundering old Barney had suddenly been transformed into a bona fide Saint Bernard rescue dog. One teenaged girl lay propped against a tree, rubbing her forehead and crying. From the marks and tracks on the gravel road, it was obvious that it had been Barney who had dragged the teenager from the crashed van. As I drew nearer, I could see Barney using his massive jaws and brute animal strength to tug a second girl from the wreckage.

I knelt beside the first girl and saw that the back of her head was bleeding. As if I had the gift of miracle healing, I told the girl that she would be all right. How I wished that I also possessed the power of prophecy—if I did I would have known enough to bring my cell phone with me so that I could call 911 and get immediate help for these girls.

Barney had wrestled the second girl free of the wreckage and was dragging her to rest beside the first teenager. I marveled at those powerful jaws that I had never seen grasp anything bigger or tougher than his rubber rat.

When I looked more closely at the second girl, it was apparent even to my layman's eyes that she had suffered a severely broken leg. She seemed, however, to be in a state of shock that temporarily placed her beyond pain.

"I need to go to call for help," I told the girl with the head wound.

She nodded, grimacing at the pain in her skull. "Just leave your dog with us, okay, mister?"

"Okay," I smiled, stooping down to rub Barney's huge head affectionately. "He is, after all, a Saint Bernard."

"Yeah," she agreed. "They're all trained to rescue people, aren't they? He sure rescued Melinda and me."

"He sure did," I grinned as I turned to run back to the house to call an ambulance and the highway patrol.

from ANIMAL MIRACLES

Rite of Passage

BRENDA RANDOLPH

Children may admire the "Taco Bell dog" on television commercials today, but in the 50's it was the big screen's Lassie that kids adored and longed for. She was a gorgeous tri-colored, full-maned collie with penetrating dark eyes that were always on alert to rescue her Timmy from certain ensuing peril. She was also always ready to comfort and befriend her little Timmy in time of need, and together the two portrayed great adventure stories that America's children have watched over and over throughout the years.

Timmy may have had his Lassie, but my brother had a male version of Lassie. Laddie, like Lassie, was all those things and more to my brother Keith. Laddie, too, was a golden collie with beautiful thick fur. Not only did my brother bury many of his childhood woes within Laddie's shiny coat, he also shared his deepest secrets with his furry friend. My brother was an avid reader and Laddie was his attentive listener.

Actually Laddie came to my brother as a puppy when Keith was only three. My older brother and parents lived in a little primitive shack that had been converted from a garage into a house. Their one-room "home" was nestled in the small logging town of Morton deep within the Cascade mountains of Washington.

My very young newlywed parents had left the Ozarks in search of work. Being only 15 and 16, without high school diplomas and money, a friend of the family put a roof over their heads by finishing out their garage for my parents. The timber industry was booming in the northwest, so in no time at all my dad found work and mother found out she was pregnant. In the middle of a snowy February winter in 1954, Keith was born. Struggling to make ends meet, time marched on for my parents, and soon my brother was celebrating his third birthday within the walls of their little home.

A next-door neighbor's female collie had just had a litter of puppies. Neighbor Bill brought one over to my family. Though Keith was still just a toddler, Bill Moe believed every boy needed a dog, and it was just a matter of time that Keith would need one, too.

Puppy and toddler soon explored as one. As usual, a puppy matures faster than a child, so it wasn't long before Laddie outgrew their favorite game. Most puppies would have bailed out of a yellow toy truck, but Laddie was ever-patient with his little pal. He rode in the back while my brother crawled along the hard linoleum floor, pushing him in his big yellow Tonka truck!

Soon Keith too had graduated from playing indoors to riding his red tricycle out in the yard. One day as the morning steam was rising over the mountains, Mother looked out the window and realized Keith was nowhere in sight. Since their house used to be a garage, there was a fence on three sides but no gate on the front. My mother began calling and searching the neighborhood. After frantically looking for what seemed like a very long time, she turned to Laddie in distress, and commanded, "Go find Keith, Laddie. I don't know where he is." The dog sensed what was wrong and took off in a flash. Hidden under some of Washington's tall Douglas firs, there was a gravel path nearby that led to my aunt's house. That was the direction Laddie ran. In just a few minutes, Laddie was seen trotting up the path with my brother's shirt sleeve in his mouth. He was tugging on boy and tricycle all the way home! Mother was so relieved that she screamed for joy and ran to meet them. This time it was she who buried her emotions in Laddie's fur. Fortunately they were tears of joy and thankfulness.

From that day on, Laddie took care of his little charge by guarding the opening in the fence. He seemed to know this was his job and he did it well. If my brother ever ventured outside the invisible line, Laddie was there to retrieve him by barking his warning and then working to turn Keith around. Mother never had to worry again.

It was the summer of 1957 and my parents decided to move "back home" to the Ozarks. Laddie was indeed a part of the family so he would go, too. Mother was pregnant with me now as they loaded what little belongings they had into a small trailer behind their old '54 Ford. They followed the roads by day and slept in their car by night. Laddie slept outside the car to keep watch over his little family.

With no air conditioning back then, crossing Nebraska and Kansas in the summer was not only unbearable for my pregnant mother, it was also miserable for Laddie with his thick heavy coat. At Dad's insistence, Mother would crawl in the back with my brother and put Laddie up front where he could get more air! Stopping only for gas, a little food and water, the three and Laddie traveled 2,300 miles together that summer.

My parents settled back in the community of their childhood at the Oregon-Shannon County line. Mother, as well as Laddie, was relieved when the oak leaves began to turn and the temperatures began to dip. It was here that I was born, and to welcome me into this world were my brother, parents, and Laddie, of course. Several of my first photos revealed my brother and Laddie peeking over the bassinet!

Though Laddie entertained many children who came to visit by letting them have a ride on his back, it was clear whose dog he really was, for he never strayed from Keith's side. My dad and grandfather were working the family sawmill nearby one day and after repeated reprimands not to go near it, my brother got too close. My dad reached out to swat him and send him to the "house." Laddie was there in a second in defense of my brother. He grabbed Dad by the arm and bit him. My dad learned a valuable lesson about disciplining my brother in front of Laddie that day!

Time was passing and it was time for Keith to board the big yellow school bus. Laddie didn't understand this rite of passage or exactly where his best buddy was going, but he would walk my brother to the end of the lane and wait with him until the bus would carry my brother away. Some days Laddie passed the time by rounding up the cows for milking, but mostly he just found a shade to lie under and waited for my brother's return. He always seemed to know the time Keith would be coming home for he'd be right back down at the end of the lane waiting. My parents always knew when the bus had arrived by the sound of Laddie's excited bark. Within just a couple of minutes, dog and boy could be seen coming up the lane. Had it not been for the round wire glasses framing my brother's face, the scene could have come right out of a scene from *Lassie*.

In the spring of 1961, at the time when my grandfather retired, my parents bought the sawmill and transferred it and our family about 30 miles south to Alton. My parents found a small tract of land at the edge of town that had a house, and in the back, wedged between house and creek bank, they expanded their business to a full-service lumberyard.

Though perhaps not too safe by today's standards, the lumberyard was playground and home for Keith, Laddie and me. Trucks hustled in and out from 8 to 5 each day so the noise and confusion became our way of life. All the while, Laddie still seemed to struggle with the hot Missouri summers and the intense heat that the 18-wheelers produced. Trying hard to help, one summer my dad even borrowed some old clippers and sheared him. Laddie may have felt much better but my brother was devastated! "His beautiful golden fur was ruined," my brother cried, as he burned hot tears of disappointment into Laddie's skin, wondering if it would ever grow back as pretty as it had been.

Laddie's temperament soon became well known with customers, friends, and truckers. Everyone loved him and referred to him as "Keith's dog." Neighbors even borrowed him for stud services. They wanted his demeanor and golden coat passed on in the bloodline of their puppies.

Right after school started one year, when the weather was still hot, Keith received a visitor to his third-grade classroom. A friend and employee of my parents brought a message that my brother was needed at home. Not understanding why Don had picked him up or why he was so visibly distraught, my brother soon learned the reason when he got home. To escape the heat of the day, Laddie had crawled under one of the lumberyard trucks. Unknowing, Don backed over something. He stopped and pulled forward, then got out to see what he had hit. It was Laddie. He choked back tears as he immediately realized the seriousness of his offense.

As my parents rushed to the scene of the accident with a blanket and bandages, they sent Don for my brother. The clatter and bustle of the day came to a screeching halt. Customers and friends alike joined round the little blond-headed boy who was grieving into his best friend's (what was now) uneven cropped hair. Though Laddie was alive and seriously injured, he tried to console his young master by licking his tears away. He tried to get up for my brother but couldn't.

My parents placed Laddie on a blanket and hoisted him into the back of the pickup. Mother drove while my brother and I rode in the back of the truck to the nearest veterinarian. With tears streaming down, Keith held Laddie's head for the entire 40-mile trip. My dad stayed behind but did phone ahead to his cousin, the veterinarian, to say we were en route.

The diagnosis was not good. Laddie's back was broken and there was nothing that could be done. Doc Ledgerwood suggested we leave him there to be put down. Mother could not make that decision. Laddie had not let her down in her time of need so she would not let him down now. Perhaps he could be "loved" back to health. It was certainly worth a try.

Returning home that evening everyone was committed to try to rehabilitate him. A sling was constructed hanging from a tree, but with no feeling in his hind quarters our efforts to get him to stand were fruitless.

Within a few days, my dad could see the end coming soon. Flies were beginning to swarm, and the heat had taken its final toll on him. Dad whispered to Mom, "If he's not gone by tomorrow, I'm going to have to do something." Not wanting to hear those words again, Mother turned away. Laddie helped them both one last time. He quietly slipped away that afternoon.

When my brother stepped off the school bus at 3:30, he

instantly noticed his buddy was gone. The place in the grass where he had lain was bare. Mom and Dad were waiting with outstretched arms. Together they walked down the hill, crossed the lumberyard to a small sycamore tree behind the old shaving house. Under the tree, there was a fresh shallow grave. With tears rolling down everyone's faces, this was one of my brother's most difficult rites of passage.

Within each one's life there will be many rites of passage, some will come harder than others. In Psalms 89:48, we learn: "What man can live and not see death." Whether it be oneself or one's best friend, we know one cannot be saved from the power of the grave. At age nine, my brother sadly discovered this powerful message.

The Animals Never Yell at Me

MICHAEL, age 10

The animals never yell at me.

The animals never make me do things

I don't want to do.

They don't expect too much of me.

They don't get mean or mad.

They're always there to run with me.

And make me feel not sad.

from ANIMAL BLESSINGS

READY TO HELP

*"Your friend is your
needs answered."*

KAHLIL GIBRAN

Want to know how to make an animal happy? Ask him or her to help you do something. Such as . . . lift your spirits when you're feeling down, get out and go for a long walk, meet new friends, plant a vegetable garden, visit someone who's sick, cram for a big test, dare to dream, and share a good laugh.

A Cat Named Hope

DEE SHEPPE

$\mathcal{W}$hen my teenage son had his first major disappointment in life, I was at a loss to help him. Rob was a senior in high school, and he felt his future closing in on him. He had spent months and all his money making a film to apply to film school—and the film had been ruined during sound editing. His girlfriend, his brother, and I tried to talk to him, but he just sat for what seemed like hours with his head in his hands. Our cat, Hope, curled at his feet.

My son's trials made me think about Hope, how she had had such a difficult start in life and had grown into the most affectionate animal in the house. She greets me at the door when I come home. She sleeps on my bed. She's at peace with everybody and helped bring a calm and peacefulness to our house, which isn't easy when you've got two teenage sons, a couple of cats and a dog!

To judge by our first meeting, I never would have guessed how much this cat would mean to our family. I'd seen her and her four kittens one day when I was volunteering at the local animal shelter. When I opened the cage to hold her, a staff member shouted a warning, "That cat is a terror!" But I saw that the mother cat was just scared in the crowded and noisy shelter and was determined to protect her babies.

Time was running out quickly on the mother and her kittens at the animal shelter. At the end of the day, I took the little family home, hoping I could foster them for a while and find them all homes later.

The mother cat was nervous and hostile in our house. When the kittens were ready, I brought the family back to the shelter for adoption. The kittens soon found good homes, but their mother wasn't so lucky—after a few days at the shelter, she got sick. I didn't know what it was about this cat, but I missed her. I took her home again from the shelter, figuring I'd nurse her back to health and put her back up for adoption. I still didn't even know her name.

But back at the shelter a third time, the mother cat, now healthy and adoptable, went ballistic! I had to get her out again! This time, I rushed to the veterinarian to have this "terror" spayed; I thought it would calm her down and make her more adoptable. I was so frustrated when I got her to the vet's that when the receptionist asked for the cat's name I blurted out, "I don't know! She's hopeless!"

Later, in the parking lot, it suddenly dawned on me. The cat had escaped the animal shelter not once, but *three* times. She'd beaten incredible odds and never gave up. Her name was obvious!

That afternoon we didn't even notice her near my son's feet. I held my breath as I watched Rob try to cope with his disappointment. At last, he stood up and stumbled, almost stepping on the cat. With a grin on his face he looked at us and said, "I almost stamped out Hope." The phrase became an inspiration in our household. Years later, we still use it on those days when we need encouragement. My son married his girlfriend, went on to film school and became a successful television producer, and our wonderful cat is still with us. All of which proves you can't stamp out Hope in this household.

from CAT CAUGHT MY HEART

Goldie, the Peking Drake

EVELYN v. K. BENHAM

$\mathcal{A}$s Mama rubbed her cheek against the newly hatched duckling, they seemed somehow to share an unknown feeling, like a bond between them. Mama wondered why, from a dozen eggs which had been put under an old setting hen, only one managed to survive.

What had happened to the others? Perhaps a 'possum or 'coon robbed the nest. However, Mama felt there was a reason for it all and, in time, her questions would be answered.

The little duckling settled down in Mama's hand and closed it's eyes. "I wonder what would be a good name for you," Mama said. "I know—your name will be Goldie, for you look as if you have been dipped in yellow paint."

The children of the family promised to help care for the little orphan.

It was still early spring, and the weather was cold and rainy. One morning Mama looked out the window and there was Goldie paddling around in a puddle of water! Mama was horrified! She had read books on ducks and knew that ducklings should not, under any circumstances, be chilled. Swimming was good and kept older ducks healthy and clean; their webbed feet were for that purpose and they enjoyed it. But Goldie was still little and not too many days ago had been hatched. So with the help of the children, Mama caught the little duck and brought it into the warm kitchen.

A box was fixed with straw and pans of warm water and crushed oatmeal, then placed behind the wood stove. Thereafter, that place remained Goldie's domain.

Every evening as night approached, Goldie started a baby duckling sleepy noise. Mama thought something was wrong, but she finally decided it meant, "lights out." From then on, the families' activities were regulated by Goldie's sleeping habits.

On warm summer days, Goldie was brought out in his box and set on the screened back porch. Little Paul, the baby of the family, at the time was also put on the porch in his playpen. Every now and then the baby got fretful, wanted attention, and started crying. The minute he began, Goldie would stand on his webbed feet, flap his wings and run up and down in his box. This amused the baby for hours on end. Goldie seemed to look forward to these outings and it was a boon for Mama. She sensed that Goldie, in his own little way, was trying to help her.

As the warm days of summer set in, the duckling had really grown. Now, some of Goldie's tail feathers turned up in a little circle at the end. That was a sign he was a drake. His neck was long and slender, and his yellow downy feathers had given way to a creamy-white plumage that glistened in the light. The body was long, broad, and deep, with a full breast. The shank and toes were reddish-brown, and when he was angry they seemed to flash out with sparks.

Goldie really felt his importance. He decided he was too old now to stay in his box and was quite capable of taking care of himself. This came as a blow to Mama, but she learned to accept it in time. From now on, Goldie stayed under the house at night.

No matter where Goldie heard Mama's voice, he cocked his head in her direction and looked with one eye. He seemed to understand everything. He was quite remarkable. Sometimes if Mama was outside and called to her pet, it wasn't long before he came running, with his beautiful wings outstretched, and flew up into her arms. All the while he would be snapping his bill as if he were talking to her.

As the ducks and chickens were fed, Goldie stayed close to Mama, and every now and then he jumped up and took the corn from her hand. This, of course, annoyed the other fowl. Consequently, they wouldn't have anything to do with Goldie. He had such a cocky air about him. Somehow he always appeared to have the upper hand.

For instance, as the dogs ate their food and things were going along fine, Goldie darted in, gulped a bill full of dog food and ran to where the dogs couldn't reach him. He would then enjoy his stolen food. He kept this up until the dogs were fighting mad and lots of times they would forget about eating and started biting and snarling at each other. This was the moment Goldie was waiting for. He then helped himself to what food was left and pretended he didn't know what was going on.

As Goldie grew, so did little Paul. One of the little boy's bad habits was to run, when no one was looking, out to the road, plunk himself down, and stuff his mouth full of gravely rocks. (I always said that was the reason Paul had such good teeth; he cut his gums on those rocks.)

Little Paul missed being run over many times by the log trucks. Time and again the family reached the road just in time to snatch him from danger. No amount of spanking and talking did any good. Mama was at her wits' end.

Somehow Goldie sensed what was going on about the boy. One day when little Paul thought no one was near, he ran as fast as his fat legs could carry him to the road. Goldie rushed after him, and began pecking at the boy's bare feet and legs. That took little Paul by surprise and for a second he was dumbfounded. As soon as he got his breath, he set up a howl that was heard a mile away. It brought the family out in all directions. "Ma-ma, Ma-ma, Goldie eat me up!" screamed the little boy. Mama picked up her little boy, brought him inside and put salve on his legs. She didn't scold him or Goldie.

Soon little Paul tried his trick again. Mama was about to run after him when she noticed that as he reached the forbidden area, there stood Goldie. He stood in the middle of the road. Little Paul didn't lose any time. He made an about face and ran toward the house with Goldie after him. Somehow he scrambled up the steps, yanked open the screen door, and slammed it shut. It was the only thing that saved him from a pecking.

The family came in to see about the commotion. Little Paul lay gasping for breath on the floor. On the porch stood Goldie, looking with glaring, angry eyes at the boy. Then he turned and waddled off with his head held high. Little Paul had learned his lesson and learned it well.

Often now, Goldie took to wandering and many times would be found in abandoned corn fields, looking for grain and rare tidbits. One morning some of Goldie's creamy-white feathers were found in the woods. No one knew what happened, but he met his end proudly, of that I am sure. The family talked long of his sweet and loving ways.

Mama kept silent. Now the questions had been answered. Mama felt Goldie had really been left for a purpose and that was to help her with little Paul. The purpose accomplished, it was time for him to go. I noticed Mama went towards the woods. I wanted to follow and comfort her, but it was best she be alone.

Now the bond, instead of being broken, was stronger than ever between Mama and Goldie.

The Wisdom of Athena

WILLIAM HENDRYX

---

*B*rian Long winced slightly as he jabbed the hypodermic needle into his arm, injecting the lifesaving insulin. He'd been a diabetic for more than half his 16 years, so it was a fairly routine chore.

When the tenth-grader glanced at his watch, he realized the school bus would arrive any minute. He said goodbye to his mother, who'd been confined to bed by an auto accident. Then he raced out the door of his family's rural home in Dunnellon, Florida. He was immediately greeted by his big seven-month-old puppy.

"Hey, Athena!" said Brian, playfully hugging the dog. "How're you doing, girl?" He'd used his own savings to acquire his pet and had named her after the Greek goddess of wisdom. Now, the two were almost inseparable.

With Athena at his side, Brian strolled down the 400-yard drive to the highway. He settled atop the drainage culvert adjacent to the road shortly after 7 A.M. to wait for the bus. Moments later, he blacked out. Athena watched as several cars passed without slowing. Then, inexplicably, the school bus did the same. As the minutes ticked by, Athena grew more anxious, licking Brian's face and whimpering. Finally, she ran onto the highway and just stood there, defiant.

Some minutes later, as Sandra Hamilton was driving to the school where she teaches, she noticed the large black dog in the middle of the road. She thought little of it until she spotted a youngster lying face down atop a drainage culvert. She continued on her way, but the image of the boy kept nagging at her. *Oh, it'll just take me a minute to check on him,* she thought, making an abrupt U-turn.

Sandra pulled onto the drive next to Brian. "Are you all right?" she called out. There was no response. An alarm went off in Sandra's head. Her mother-in-law had been diabetic, and she knew the signs of insulin shock.

Suddenly fearful, Sandra sped up the long driveway, horn blaring. A small, sleepy-eyed girl answered the door, then led Sandra to her mother. When Brian's brother, Kevin, heard the news, he got some apple juice and ran to Brian's side, while Sandra phoned for help.

When paramedics arrived, Brian was coming to, thanks to the fruit juice and the kisses of his four-legged pal. He'd been unconscious for 45 minutes and might have gone into a coma and died if not for Sandra and Athena. He later admitted that he hadn't eaten enough breakfast, which triggered the attack.

from WOMAN'S DAY

Hero Mom

KATHRYN LAY

"You're my hero, Mom," my six-year-old daughter said.

"I am?" My heart swelled. What had I done to merit such a statement? I knew my daughter was enraptured by certain cartoon figures, enjoyed a few sports figures, and read certain authors voraciously.

"Remember Cheep-Cheep?" she asked. "You stopped and saved him."

I nodded.

"And the kitten in the road?"

I nodded again. I could see where she was heading. In the last six months, I'd rescued a few wayward animals.

Cheep-Cheep was a small baby bird, lying in the middle of the road, near the train tracks. I had dropped my daughter off at Vacation Bible School and was heading home to write and relax for a couple of hours. But on the road, I saw the bird trying to hop between the cars. I slammed on my brakes, backed up and ran to the helpless creature. Drivers honked and I held my hand out like a policeman, commanding them to stop. It took a little dancing to capture the creature. I scooped it into my hands and into my car before fleeing the busy road.

When my daughter returned from Vacation Bible School, she was amazed at my story. We took care of the bird the best we knew how. After calling a few bird rehabilitators in the area, we finally found one able to take the baby, but not until Monday. This was Friday.

Together, we kept the baby warm and fed it water with an eye dropper. It wasn't easy to let Cheep-Cheep go, and Michelle cried. But apparently, I was still a hero.

I often feel unamazing in my daughter's eyes. I don't wear a business suit to work. Or a uniform. Or even a clown outfit. Instead, I sit in slacks or shorts while teaching homeschool, becoming even less formal while writing at the computer. We're together a lot. But she reminds me of the times I have helped animals.

There have been many rescues with injured or helpless animals. We've stopped on the road to snatch a kitten from certain harm. We've watched "Lost Dog" signs, searching for the missing animal in hopes of returning it to a lonely family. We've moved dazed turtles from a busy road to a nearby pond.

Cheep-Cheep made me a hero in Michelle's eyes. We both love and respect the variety of animals, birds, and sea creatures God has given us to enjoy.

"Can I do anything I want when I grow up?" she asks. "Even though I'm a girl?"

I nod vigorously. "Anything you want."

She thinks a moment. I know there are lots of ideas in her head about the many jobs she'd like to have. Whatever it is, I'm sure one day, she'll be a hero, too. To her own daughter. To young girls around her. To the many animals that cross her path.

And, especially, to her Mom.

Sosha: Therapy Ferret

KATHY SMITH

I have a very special pet ferret named Sosha. I know all people think their pets are special, but Sosha has done something pretty remarkable—especially for a ferret.

A few months ago, a friend of mine brought her mentally disabled four-year-old son, Marc, over to my house for a visit. Now Sosha is very wary of strangers. Also, he doesn't usually stay awake more than an hour or two at a time. But when Marc sat down on the floor, Sosha immediately walked over to the boy and allowed the child to hold and inspect him. He didn't try to play with Marc or to run away as he usually does. Instead, he remained uncharacteristically passive. It was so strange because I'd never seen my ferret allow himself to be held that long. By anyone. He doesn't even let *me* hold him for more than two minutes to be petted.

Sosha seemed to sense that there was something different about this child. He just continued to let Marc pet and hold him. Then, all of a sudden, the boy looked up and blurted out "cat!" It was the first time any of us had heard him speak a single word! My four-year-old daughter tried explaining to Marc that Sosha was a ferret and not a cat. But he didn't care— and neither did his mother or I. We were so excited that he had said something. Sosha had reached him somehow, and made a connection. Marc now comes over every week for "ferret therapy."

I don't know if it's that Sosha is a special ferret or just that Marc believes he is, but there is a bond between the two that is inexplicable. I've heard stories before about dogs making a connection with people who are afflicted with different disorders, but I never dreamed a ferret could do the same. In fact, Sosha now seems to know when Marc is coming over and stays awake and with him whenever he's here.

Since that first breakthrough moment, Marc has come remarkably far with his speech. He now makes a genuine effort to talk to the ferret. He still calls him a cat, but I don't think Sosha minds one bit! And as far as I'm concerned, a healing animal by any name is still a miracle worker.

from HEART SONGS FOR ANIMAL LOVERS

Pepper Catches the Burglars

ROBERTA SANDLER

---

*J*odi was so excited about her shiny new 10-speed bicycle, she could barely wait until her official 12th birthday the following day. My husband and I had bought the bike for her and tried to hide it in the garage, but our daughter spotted it and grinned with delight. She had wanted it for a long time.

Our pet cat, Pepper, a five-year-old black alley cat who had followed Jodi home from school when he was a mere kitten, seemed unimpressed with the bike. Still, when Jodi snuggled under her bedcovers with Pepper that night, she whispered to him, "Maybe I'll put you in the basket and take you for a ride tomorrow."

It was around 2 a.m. when Pepper awakened. Jodi stirred. Despite her closed eyes, she sensed that something had caught Pepper's attention. My daughter heard the sound of thunder. The cat had never reacted to rain and thunder, so Jodi was surprised when she opened her eyes and saw that Pepper had leaped from the bed, and climbed onto the desk in front of Jodi's bedroom window. The window overlooked our garage. Jodi was now fully aroused from her sleep. She watched Pepper as he stared intently at something outside the window. He pawed the window and meowed.

Jodi again heard the sound. "It's only thunder," she told Pepper. Or was it? Curious, she got out of bed and went to look out her window. There, to her fright and amazement, she saw two men guiding her bike out of the garage and down the driveway between my husband's and my cars. It wasn't two claps of thunder she had heard, after all. It was the sound of the unlocked garage door being raised and then lowered.

My husband Marty and I were awakened from a sound sleep by our daughter.

"Dad, wake up!" she implored, while shaking my husband's shoulder. Pepper stood by our bed, close to Jodi.

"What? What is it?" Marty mumbled.

"Two guys are stealing my bike!" she exclaimed. "They took my bike from the garage!"

"You must be dreaming," I said.

"No," Jodi insisted. "I saw them. I mean, Pepper saw them. He heard them opening the garage door."

With that, Marty jumped out of bed, quickly donned his trousers, and reached for the gun he was licensed to carry. Sliding his feet into a pair of loafers, he ran down the stairs and out of the house. I dialed 911.

"Stay here," I instructed Jodi after I had phoned the police. I ran out of the house, but I looked back and saw Pepper staring out of the living-room window. He seemed to want to know what was going on.

I rushed from the driveway to the curb, and glanced left and right, but couldn't find Marty or the two burglars. And then I saw them, way down toward the corner of the street. Marty had had to run fast to catch up with them. I caught up to them and stood behind my husband. He had his gun pointed at them. It was the only way to keep them in sight until the police arrived.

I could see that the burglars had desperately tried to hide Jodi's bike in the bushes of a front yard, once they realized that Marty was after them. The handlebars, gleaming in the moonlight, stuck out from the bushes.

"C'mon, man," one of the burglars pleaded. "I can't go to jail. I have a new baby to take care of." His eyes looked glassy, as though he had been drinking. He waved a beer bottle as he spoke. I thought, *All he has to do is break the glass, and the bottle becomes a deadly weapon.* The second burglar kept his hands up over his head.

We later learned that the burglar did not have a new baby, and wasn't even married. He had simply tried to appeal to our sympathies.

I was livid. "That bicycle was a birthday present for my daughter! How dare you violate our privacy? How dare you break into our home and steal a child's bike?"

The burglars tried to convince us that it was just a prank. A prank? Tell that to a heartbroken child whose only wish was to have a new, 10-speed bike.

A police car pulled up. The officer arrested the burglars. It was the beginning of an emotional ordeal in which we eventually had to appear in court as witnesses. The bike was taken as evidence in the court trial.

It seemed somewhat ludicrous to me that as part of my testimony, I had to tell the jury that our family cat was the primary witness, for it was Pepper who had seen it all, and who had alerted Jodi that something was wrong. The jurors smiled. A cat? Yes. Our hero cat.

The jurors were not permitted to know that the two burglars had an arms-length list of prior offenses, and had served prison time. Therefore, if the two men were found guilty, they would receive about a 7-10-year prison sentence. For stealing a bike? No, that was too harsh a punishment just for a bike, the jurors thought. And they acquitted the burglars. The acquittal was devastating to Jodi and frustrating to Marty and me. The burglars, unkempt and high on alcohol when they committed their crime, were now clean-shaven and dressed in suits, which further convinced the jurors that these two nice-looking young men shouldn't go to prison.

The trial ended, and Jodi was allowed to reclaim her bike. As for the burglars, "It's unfair," she told us. We had to explain that sometimes the legal system works and sometimes it doesn't. And after the trial, several jurors exclaimed: "If only we had known."

When we returned home from the courthouse, Jodi took Pepper in her arms. She carried him to the garage, which we vowed would forever after be locked, and she stroked the cat's fur.

"This is my bike," she told Pepper. "I almost lost it, but you got it back for me, Pepper. You saved my birthday. Thank you, Pepper." The feline gloried in the kisses that Jodi lavishly bestowed upon him.

Our beloved, modest cat never knew that he had become a hero to our family and to the neighborhood children. But for the rest of his life, Pepper was known locally as "the cat who caught the burglars."

Sweet Shiva

ROBIN KOVARY

$\mathcal{S}$hiva was an exceptionally sweet, affectionate, and well-behaved female Bull Mastiff. We worked together for many years. I'll never forget one visit in particular that involved a special little girl. Shiva and I had already been volunteering for several months in the pediatrics division of a large New York hospital. Many of the children there had serious, life-threatening diseases. Each month, Shiva and I visited this hospital together, hoping to give these young patients a way to get their minds off their worries and pain for at least a little while. The children who were ambulatory were allowed to walk Shiva through the halls of the hospital. They loved the smiles and attention they received from the doctors and nurses who passed them. Other children would brush Shiva's brindle coat, pet her soft ears, or have their photographs taken with her.

There was one child, however, who never once spoke, interacted, or showed us anything but the saddest of facial expressions during our visits. She was about six years old, very thin, and had no hair left because of her extensive chemotherapy treatments. I was told that she was in the advanced stages of cancer and that she was both physically and emotionally depressed. The staff told me that she rarely spoke to anyone anymore, not even to her caregivers at the hospital, despite their best efforts to draw her out.

Around the fourth month into our pet therapy visits, Shiva herself was diagnosed with cancer and had to undergo extensive surgery. She was unable to visit the children for more than a month. When Shiva was fully recovered, we resumed our visits. The children wanted to know why we hadn't come the month before. I explained that Shiva had cancer, that she had to have surgery, and that she needed time to heal before she was able to come back and visit them. Well, suddenly the little girl with no hair lit up! For the first time in all those months, she flooded us with questions: Was Shiva going to lose her hair? Was she going to die?

The staff members were amazed. More than a dozen hospitalized children in the room became more animated, full of curiosity about the dog who shared their illness. And I was told afterward by a nurse that Shiva's visit was enormously helpful in allowing them to reach the seemingly unreachable little girl. Less than one year later, Shiva died of a ruptured heart-based tumor. Shiva's registered name, given to her as a puppy, was "Guardian Angel." She certainly lived up to it.

from ANIMALS AS TEACHERS & HEALERS

A Spark of Life

BRAD STEIGER AND SHERRY HANSEN STEIGER

It seemed especially appropriate to Naiomi Johnston that she would give birth to her daughter on Valentine's Day, February 14, 1993. And while she was recuperating in the hospital, her husband Darryl and their three-year-old son Donald were at home in Midland, Ontario, surrounded by snowdrifts, eagerly anticipating the return of mother and brand-new baby sister.

Little Donald was eager to see his mommy and his baby sister. He really missed Mommy, and he just couldn't wait to see what a sister would look like.

Daddy told him that he had to wait awhile. It was very cold outside, and there were snowdrifts as high as mountains. Travel, he had said sternly, was out of the question.

But Donald couldn't imagine that those snowbanks could stop his little electric toy car. He could see no reason why he couldn't just get into his own little car and drive off to the hospital and visit Mommy and sister. If Daddy didn't want to go, well, he could just wait at home.

Just in case Daddy might object to his setting out to visit Mommy and baby sister, Donald got up really early, while Daddy was still sleeping, and set out in his electric car to drive to the hospital.

It didn't take long for the car's battery to run down, and pretty soon it wouldn't move at all.

Not to worry. It couldn't be that far to the hospital. He would walk the rest of the way.

Once he started walking, it didn't take Donald very long to realize that Daddy was right. It really was very, very cold. And the snowdrifts were as high as mountains.

And he was lost. He had no idea where he was.

Constable Kirk Wood of the Ontario Provincial Police told journalist Esmond Choueke that at this point little Donald Johnston was probably less than thirty minutes from death. The three-year-old boy had no real protection from the cold, blowing wind.

But Donald apparently had two guardian angels on duty that cold morning in Ontario—one from heaven and another from a nearby farm.

Brian Holmes was outside his farmhouse doing chores with Samantha, his six-year-old German shepherd, when he noticed that the big dog was acting strangely, as if she sensed something was wrong. All of a sudden, she lifted her head, sniffed the air, and ran toward the woods.

Although Samantha's actions were somewhat peculiar, Holmes finally concluded that she had picked up the scent of a rabbit or some other animal, and he went on with his morning chores.

If Samantha had been able to explain her motives to her master, she might have informed him that she had far more serious concerns on that frigid morning than chasing rabbits through the snow. A sense beyond her physical sensory abilities had told her that somewhere a small human child was in a desperate situation.

Samantha found the three-year-old sitting under a tree, cold and crying. She licked his face and nudged him to his feet. She knew that the little human must not rest in any one place for very long or he would freeze to death. She kept him on his feet and continued to push him in the direction of the farmhouse.

To Donald's eyes, Samantha must have seemed like a big, furry angel. He threw his arms around her neck and allowed her to guide him along whatever path she felt was best. To his three-year-old mind, the trees bending and moaning in the cold wind and the eight-foot-high snowdrifts must have seemed like a frozen nightmare. But somehow he knew that this big dog would bring him back to warmth and life.

Brian Holmes had just begun to wonder about his German shepherd when he spotted her coming down the road with a small boy hanging on to her for dear life. He immediately brought Donald inside the farmhouse, fed him, and let him get nice and warm.

The farmer gave his dog an affectionate scratch behind her ear. Somehow, in a mysterious way beyond his ability to ascertain, Samantha had been able to sense that there was a little lost boy somewhere out there among the snowdrifts and the freezing cold. She had found Donald, and in that marvelous expression of symbiotic relationship between humans and canines, she brought him to their home so her master could keep him warm and preserve his spark of life.

from ANIMAL MIRACLES

The Kiddos

MARY JANE STRETCH

I find it hard to say no to anyone who reaches out for help. Consequently, it was inevitable that a few damaged young people also got rehabilitated along with the animals.

During my early days as a rehabber, when I was a single mother of three little girls, I worked full time at a nature center in Bucks County, Pennsylvania. I was an assistant naturalist and spent most of my time with groups of children and young people. I worked with them outdoors, acquainting them with trees, flowers, birds, and animals, many of which they saw every day yet had never noticed. The center was a popular gathering place for teenagers, perhaps because the natural world was less threatening than the world of people. Some of the young people were on the staff, some were volunteers, and some simply needed to get away from their troubles.

I wasn't hired to work with animals, but I took some of my patients with me in my car and brought their cages into my office so that I could maintain their frequent feeding schedules. To young people, that made me seem different, and when word got around that I had a house full of birds and animals, they began to bombard me with questions. One day they kept me overtime, and I wanted to get home before my daughters finished school. "Can we talk tomorrow?" I asked. "I really have to go home."

One of them said, "Can we come with you? We'd like to see your animals."

"Sure," I said, getting into my car. "Follow me."

When we arrived at the small, steep-roofed house I rented, I invited them in to talk while I fed the animals and checked on the progress of those that were recovering from injuries. When Debbie, Leah, and Sammy came home, they pitched right in, and our visitors were obviously impressed when they saw that my daughters could handle the patients as well as I could. They asked questions constantly, wanting to know what we were doing and why.

"I thought birds ate bread," Jenny said while I fed a sparrow. She kept shaking her long, tangled brown hair away from her face as she bent down for a closer look. She was one of the kids who hung out at the center, just watching, never getting involved. This was the first time I had heard her speak. Usually she let her friend Kevin do all the talking.

"Bread has no nutritional value for them," I explained. "Most birds eat seeds, fruit, or insects."

"Why?"

"It depends on their beaks," Leah said, lifting a chipmunk out of its cage and inspecting a foot that had been infected. "Some beaks aren't built to handle seeds."

"Then how do they eat?"

"They go someplace where they can find bugs," Debbie said matter-of-factly. She glanced at me with a question in her eyes. She was reminding me that it was nearly time to make dinner. Were these kids going to stay? And if so, what on earth would we feed them?

Those were hard times for us financially. We lived on my modest salary and a small trust fund from my late husband.

There was only enough money for the four of us, but I was also feeding a growing number of birds and animals, and in our house, the animals came first. We always ate, but our menu was simple. To this day, Debbie cannot stand tuna fish and Leah won't even look at an egg, because during those early years they were the mainstays of our diet. "I know, Mom," Debbie used to say, rolling her eyes when I put another tuna casserole on the dinner table. "It's good protein. I know."

We had five visitors: Jenny and Kevin; Joan, who worked at the center; and Denise and Hank, both volunteers. Mentally I took an inventory of my cupboard and decided that we didn't have enough tuna fish. But we did have some cans of soup.

Denise and Hank were expected home for dinner and left, but the others lingered. When I said, "How about some food?" they accepted eagerly.

"Okay," I said, "but you'll have to earn it." Some of our cages needed cleaning, and if the kids could do it, that would save me time later in the evening. Usually I went to bed after feeding the baby animals at eleven o'clock. Then I got up at 3 A.M. and 7 A.M. to feed them again. With a little more help, I might get more sleep.

The kids were all smiles as they went straight to work on the cages, with Debbie as supervisor. Debbie was thirteen, and I think it made her feel important to be able to instruct kids who were a few years older, because in the teen years even a few months can make a difference in status. She showed Jenny and Kevin how to handle the animals while removing them from their cages, and although they were hesitant at first, for fear of hurting them, they learned quickly. Meanwhile, Leah and I finished our feeding and warmed up the soup.

A few days earlier, I had come home with two baby great

horned owls that a man had found and brought in to the center because he heard that I was licensed to take care of them. They were too big for any of my cages, so I made a nest out of a roasting pan and put straw in it. The owls snuggled into it quite comfortably, and since I was running out of counter and floor space, I spread newspapers in the middle of the kitchen table and set the pan on top of them. My daughters and I were accustomed to such things, but to our guests it was a novelty.

"Hey, what kind of soup is this?" Kevin teased. "I found a feather in it!" He held up a dripping feather that once had been fluffy and white and now was the color of Campbell's vegetable beef.

"We always have feathers in our soup," Sammy said, as if it were an honor. She was particularly fond of owls.

"It's a garnish!" Leah said, giggling, and we all laughed.

After dinner, the kids helped us clear the table and do the dishes. They didn't seem to want to leave, and I saw no reason to push them out. I knew that Joan tried to spend as little time at home as possible because there was friction between her and her father's new wife. I knew nothing about Kevin and Jenny or their families.

I started a fire in the living room, and we sat on the floor in front of it, talking about animals. My daughters were getting sleepy, and it was almost time for them to go to bed, but they enjoyed the company of young people who didn't talk down to them. After they went upstairs, the rest of us began to sing a folk song that was popular at the time. Two of the kids had marvelous voices and the rest of us didn't, but that didn't matter. One song led to another, and soon it was time for my eleven o'clock feeding. I didn't get any extra sleep, but I felt relaxed, and that was a gift in itself. "I've got work to do," I said, heading for the kitchen. "Then I'm going to bed. You can stay over, if you want, but I don't have any extra beds."

"Thanks, Mom," Jenny said. "The floor will be fine." Although she and I weren't many years apart, she went on calling me Mom. It caught on with some of the other young people, too. To the others I was M. J.

I had several baby raccoons, and feeding them took a long time. First I would heat the formula, exactly as I would for a human baby, and then I'd play with the coons for a while to get them moving around. I would wrap the baby coons one at a time in a towel or a diaper and hold it in my arms while I gave it a bottle. Halfway through the bottle, I would put the coon over my shoulder and burp it. I knew that if I didn't get the gas bubbles out, I would have crying babies within an hour. Their natural mother wouldn't have had to worry about burping them because while her babies were nursing, they'd be bumping into their siblings, and that would take care of their gas.

As usual, the feeding was a slow process. If the babies didn't eat well for me at first—because my formula didn't taste like their mother's—I had to teach them how to take the milk by working their little mouths around the nipple. Getting a certain amount of formula into them was crucial to their survival.

After they were fed, the coons had to be pottied, often by stimulating them with a warm cloth or paper towels. Then I did what any raccoon mother would have done: I washed their faces and behinds. After the coons, I went on to the other animals. I didn't have to feed the birds, because they don't eat at night. The owls did, but they had a bedroom all to themselves on the second floor, and I brought them some cut-up cockerels I got for nothing at a poultry processing plant.

By midnight I was finished. I had been so intent on the animals that I hadn't noticed how quiet the living room was, and when I looked in, I saw Joan asleep on the couch and Jenny and Kevin in sleeping bags on the floor. I turned off the lights and went to bed. When I got up for my 3 A.M. feeding, everyone was still sound asleep.

My mornings were always hectic. I had to feed my patients at seven o'clock, make our breakfast, and see my daughters off to school. Then I would dress and go to work, taking some of the animals with me. I had no time for house guests. But when I looked at the three slumbering teenagers in my living room, I didn't see house guests; I saw manpower.

"Up! Up! Everybody up!" I shouted, marching through the room like a drill sergeant. They were startled but still groggy as I began to negotiate a deal. I needed help, I told them, and they needed breakfast. So—I would cook a big breakfast if they would help me feed my patients. They agreed. In fact, they were happy to help. They liked animals, and it made them feel good about themselves when they could do something for them.

After breakfast, I watched my daughters get on the school bus, and then Joan and I left for the nature center. Kevin and Jenny rumbled off in Kevin's Volkswagen.

When I arrived home later that day, the Volkswagen was parked in my driveway. Kevin and Jenny were sitting on my front steps. "What's for dinner?" Kevin said, a little self-consciously.

"We want to help you with the feeding," Jenny explained.

"In exchange for dinner?" I asked.

"Yeah—sort of," Kevin said. "But you don't have to. We'd just like to feed the animals."

"Terrific!" I said. "I really can use your help—and I'd like you to stay for dinner."

They followed me into the house and headed straight for the kitchen. "You'll have to show us how to do it," Jenny said. "Debbie said if you don't feed them right, they might choke to death. Is that true?"

"Yes," I said. "But I'm not going to ask you to feed them until you learn how. For now, you can just follow me around and watch what I do. I don't know any other way to teach you."

When Debbie, Leah, and Sammy came home, they found Kevin and Jenny looking over my shoulder while I put some food into a blue jay's mouth. "You don't want to push it down the throat," I said. "Just put it in the mouth, a little bit at a time. Give the bird a chance to swallow it. If you push the food all the way to the back of the throat, it might go into the windpipe."

Understandably, my girls were happy to have two more pairs of hands. They worked very hard helping me take care of the house and the animals, because I didn't have any choice but to make demands on them. There was only so much I could do because I had a job, and I needed the job because we needed the money. I was well aware that my daughters didn't have some of the material things most of their friends had, and they had very little time for fun. But they didn't complain. In fact, some of their friends thought there was something special about them because they had animal friends.

When it was time for us to eat, Kevin said, "Let's get some pizza!" I scrounged in my pocketbook and came up with three dollars. "It's a start," I said, putting them on the table. "How much have you got?" I asked Kevin. He dug five crumpled singles out of various pockets and put them on top of mine. Debbie contributed a dollar she had saved from money she earned cleaning a neighbor's horse stalls.

"Okay, okay, don't make me feel guilty," Jenny moaned. She took off her shoe and threw a five-dollar bill on the pile.

"That's enough for a feast," I said, counting up fourteen dollars. That evening we dined on two pizzas and an antipasto salad and didn't leave a crumb.

We had another evening of singing and laughter, and when it was time for the eleven o'clock feeding, Kevin and Jenny offered to do it if I would watch them closely. They were good students and were starting to feel confident. "Can we solo tomorrow night?" Jenny asked.

"Why not tomorrow morning?" I said. "Be here by seven and I'll make breakfast when you're done." If they could feed the mammals while I took care of the birds, my morning would be a thing of beauty.

From then on there were always "kiddos," as we called them, in our house, and with them came music and fun. Joan joined us often, and Jenny and Kevin brought some of their friends. With their help I was able to handle more patients, and although the work was hard, we all seemed to thrive on it.

I could see the kids changing. Though their stories were different, they had one thing in common: They saw themselves as losers because they had missed out on the love and attention we all need in order to feel good about ourselves. Looking dirty and disheveled, failing when others were achieving, and breaking rules were their ways of thumbing their noses at society because that's what they accused society of doing to them. They didn't trust because they didn't feel trusted, and quite often they were right. People could choose to ignore kids like them. Animals that needed help could not. A possum, a rabbit, a sparrow, a hawk, a muskrat, or any other wild creature fighting to stay alive didn't care who owned the hand that reached out to help it. If the hand couldn't heal, the animal died, without even a murmur of blame or accusation. And if the animal survived, it went on its way without a word of thanks or approval. Results were all that counted; who you were didn't matter. Nothing could be taken personally, neither failure nor success, and for these kiddos it was like starting their lives over.

I suspect that some of the kids started helping me with my animals out of boredom and because they thought I was doing something unusual. But it became a serious effort with them because, as they grew more competent, they began to like themselves. And as their self-esteem developed, they changed the way they presented themselves to the world. From the beginning, I had made it clear that in our house there were rules. We kept ourselves clean, we didn't smoke or use drugs, we shared the work, we shared our money, and if you didn't pay for something, it wasn't yours. At first, however, I had to remind some of the kiddos to take a shower or get a haircut or return some little luxury they had slipped into a pocket while browsing through a store. To them I probably seemed old-fashioned, but they went along with me because they wanted to continue working with the animals. After a while, I didn't have to bother reminding them, because they wanted to be and look like the persons they felt themselves becoming. Instead of living from one hour to the next, they began to think about their future. Of course, once that happened, I knew they would soon be leaving. It would be like saying good-bye to baby birds when they learn to fly. . . .

It's hard for me to keep track of our kiddos because, like our animals, they go off in different directions. I don't always have telephone numbers where I can contact them, but I think about them always, and they seem to know that. Jenny called me one Christmastime after years of silence, and it was almost as if she were still here doing the eleven o'clock feeding with me. She told me she had finished an enlistment in the army and was about to get married. She sounded very happy.

"Remember how tired we used to get?" she said. "That was hard work!"

"I know," I told her. "I couldn't have done it without you."

"It meant a lot to me," she said, and I could hear her sniffing back some tears. "Say hello to your wild things for me, will you?"

I almost did some sniffing of my own. "Why don't you come and say it yourself?" I said.

"I'm going to do that," she promised. "It'll be good for me."

Sometimes our birds and animals come back for a little while, too, but that doesn't mean they can't make it out there in the wild. They just have to regain their strength and try again. Maybe it's the same with kiddos. Getting hurt or feeling that they aren't loved shakes their confidence. But when they come back to a place where they feel they have some value, they remember who they are. Animals can do that for people.

from FOR THE LOVE OF WILD THINGS

Bringing Kids Into the Flock

DR. SHARON OTIS

$\mathcal{I}$ work with troubled children and their families in a Christian family-care counseling center in Bradenton, Florida. Many of these children or adolescents refuse to talk and trust no one, their feelings "frozen" behind layers of emotional pain. Their parents often say the children won't talk at all—to anyone.

But that all changes when Obie and Tobie are on the scene. Obie (Obadiah) is a 5-year-old female chocolate Lab, and Tobie is an Old English sheepdog just a year old. I first realized the therapeutic potential of my dogs when Obie, as a pup, greeted a teenage boy in the reception area on her way out to go for a walk. When that boy came into his counseling session, he began telling me of a sad, abusive childhood. He said he never told anyone, but somehow the dog made him feel comfortable enough to open up.

So, I started working with Obie more and more. And when Tobie came along, I trained him to work with the patients, too. Positive responses to the dogs are almost immediate. The unconditional love they provide helps people with low self-esteem. The dogs are calming for hyperactive children, and they help cheer up patients who struggle with depression or have so much sadness in their lives. Mainly, they work with the young patients, but they've given me many surprises with adult patients, too.

from PETS: PART OF THE FAMILY

Two Strays
and a Miracle

KRISTIN VON KREISLER

$\mathcal{L}$ate one chilly afternoon, Josh Carlyle, a ten-year-old child with Down's syndrome, saw two stray mutts—one mostly dachshund and the other mostly blue heeler—hanging around his rural Missouri home. Fascinated by the dogs, he followed them into the rugged Ozark woods and realized too late that he did not know the way home.

When Josh's mother looked out her kitchen window to call him for supper, the boy was nowhere in sight. She went outside, shouting his name, and searched the neighborhood but could not find him. Frightened, she telephoned Sheriff Ralph Hendrix, who came immediately. As the sky darkened and the temperature fell, Hendrix knew he had a crisis on his hands.

He parked his sky-blue school bus down the hill from Josh's house and set up a command post for the search. Within a few hours, three hundred volunteers, who had heard on Hendrix's scanner that Josh was missing, showed up to help. Reserve deputies arrived. Tracking dogs were brought in from neighboring counties. All night long Hendrix sent teams of eight to ten people to comb the hills, fingertip-to-fingertip, for Josh.

When he hadn't been found by the next morning, Hendrix tried not to feel discouraged. Yet he couldn't help but fear that Josh might be dead. He sent out more volunteers and asked them to search not only the woods, but also the caves and cliff ledges. By the second night, the temperature had fallen to below zero, and no one had found any trace of Josh except for one boot print. Hendrix was worried that Josh had frozen to death overnight.

"Go north. Unless you find Josh, don't come back till dark," Hendrix told searchers on horseback the next morning.

One of the men, Oscar Nell, rode into the woods. When he tugged his horse's reins to direct him up a hill, the horse balked and insisted on turning down toward a hollow. Nell decided that the horse might know more than *he* did about Josh's whereabouts, and he let the horse lead.

Nell heard a dog barking and squinted through the distant trees in the direction of the sound. A blue heeler mutt was yapping and running up and down a steep hill; then it stopped and panted. Nell was certain that the dog was trying to get his attention.

He followed the dog deeper into the woods and discovered Josh lying on the ground. Huddled next to him was the stray dachshund.

"Josh! Josh!" Nell leaped off his horse and ran toward the boy.

The blue heeler snapped and growled at him so fiercely that Nell stopped cold. Though the stray had tried to make Nell follow him, now he appeared to consider the man a threat. Nell talked softly to the stray and tried to make his voice sound gentle, but compelling. The mutt was still reluctant to trust him but finally quit barking and seemed less inclined to bite.

When the boy raised his head, Nell was immensely relieved to see that he was still alive. Nell helped him to a sitting
position and propped him against a tree.

"Are you hungry?" Nell asked.

Josh was too cold and frightened to respond.

Nell gave him a sandwich, but Josh's chattering teeth pre-
vented him from eating. His mouth was bloody. He was covered with dirt and bits of leaves and grass. But his face was
clean, though chapped in spots where the dachshund stray
had licked him.

Nell helped Josh drink a little water, put him on the horse,
and climbed on the saddle behind him. As the horse headed
back to the search team command post, the strays protec-
tively followed.

Then Nell had to stop his horse. Josh's toes had been frost-
bitten to blisters; the jostling caused too much pain for him to
go on. Nell made a temporary camp and built a fire.

"I'll bring back help," he promised.

As he rode off, the dogs moved closer to Josh. They
guarded and warmed him until the rescue party returned in a
Jeep to take him to a helicopter.

They carefully laid him on the back seat and sped down
the road. The dogs barked and howled, clearly upset that Josh
was leaving. The dachshund chased after the car until she
could no longer keep up on her squat little legs.

Later, the strays apparently split up and wandered back to
Josh's house to look for him. A search-and-rescue volunteer
picked up the dachshund; Josh's next-door neighbors found
the heeler on a nearby hill and put out food to lure him closer.
After a veterinarian examined the strays and determined that
they were healthy, Josh's parents agreed to adopt them.

The afternoon the dogs were to join their new family, Hendrix brought them to greet Josh on his release from the hospital. The dogs, wild with excitement to see Josh again, tugged at their leads. Josh was thrilled.

The dachshund leaped onto Josh's wheelchair, licked him, and whimpered. The heeler, more reserved, sniffed Josh from head to toe to make certain that he was safe.

Their obvious devotion deeply moved Hendrix. "The Lord had them stay with Josh and take care of him," the sheriff said. "His surviving was a miracle."

A miracle made possible by the compassion of two strays.

from THE COMPASSION OF ANIMALS

He Had a Job to Do

NANCY TOMAZIC

When I was ten years old, my family was given a German Shepherd. He'd been trained as a police dog, but apparently his performance had been unsatisfactory, and he was going to be put to sleep. The dog warden, who just happened to know my father, asked if we'd like to adopt him. His name was Kazon, and he was two years old.

As it turned out, Kazon adopted us. There were four kids in my family at that time, ranging in age from toddler to teenager, and Kazon assumed responsibility for all four of us. He would follow closely behind us during the day, and at night he'd lie faithfully by the back door, guarding us against intruders. Kazon never closed his eyes. I used to sneak downstairs at night, just to see if I could catch him sleeping, but he always had one eye open. Kazon took his job very seriously.

Apart from Kazon, we had a true menagerie of animals. There were always a few horses in the barn, along with a collection of chickens, ducks, turkeys, cats, and whatever other animals happened to turn up. In the house, we kept a macaw who spoke fluently, and mimicked everyone's voice to perfection. There was the pet monkey, Buddy, who went with me everywhere, perched on my shoulder, with his long arms securely wrapped around my neck. And always, but always, there was Kazon. Unfortunately, Kazon was often taken for granted, since he wasn't nearly as entertaining as some of our more exotic animals. More often than not, Kazon was just there, watching over us, making sure we didn't get into trouble.

At breakfast one morning, my mother surprised me with the news that my riding horse, Star, had given birth to a colt. I was ecstatic, and rushed out to the barn to greet our newest family member. Kazon ran at my side, but I was oblivious to his presence. I saw Star grazing out in the pasture, and, by her side, her new colt. I ran as fast as I could, shouting joyously at Star. I leaped over the split rail fence, and continued running toward my horse. I was too excited to realize that my excitement seemed threatening to Star. She didn't like the way I was rushing at her new baby. Star laid her ears straight back and charged. Within seconds, Star was rearing up in front of me, her hooves coming down toward my head.

It was all happening so fast, I didn't have time to react. I can only remember a tremendous fear coursing through my body, realizing that I was about to die. Then, just as suddenly, I was sitting there in the middle of the pasture, wondering why I was still alive. The mare was running back toward her newborn colt. And Kazon was at my side. He'd rushed at the 1,200 lb. horse, forcing her to veer away from me.

Kazon, the dog we took for granted, was there by my side, acting as if nothing special had happened. For Kazon, it was just another day. He had a job to do, and he was doing it well.

Today, forty-two years later, I have another German Shepherd at my side. Her name is Bucky. She is my constant guardian and companion, and she is never taken for granted.

SHARING THE FUN

"And so it is you cheer me,
My old friend. . . ."

JAMES WHITCOMB RILEY

Sometimes we take life too seriously. Our animal friends know that, which is why they're always ready to take a break and have a good time. It's not that they're frivolous. But they understand that we can do our work much better if we season it with a little fun.

The Submarine

SHARON HUNTINGTON

"*D*on't bother them, and they won't bother you." My grand-mother's philosophy for getting along with animals was straight-forward. But my brother and I, unwilling to settle for such an isolationist view, developed numerous variations to this rule.

We lived on the edge of town, surrounded by animals. In one direction were houses, paved streets, and eventually the short row of stores that made up the main street of our small town. But sheep grazed in the field behind our backyard fence. Beyond them were fields, some with grazing horses or cows, then the foothills of the Rocky Mountains, filled with wildlife.

The sheep would glance at us as we crossed their field, but if we didn't appear to be carrying anything edible, they ignored us. We never entered a field with a bull. They will bother you even if you don't bother them. We could sometimes bribe an occasional horse to take a piece of apple from our hands. Dogs that were tied up or fenced were left alone. Dogs on the loose could be allowed to approach.

After sufficient sniffing on their part and reassurance on ours, lasting friendships were formed. We played with garden snakes but never brought them in the house (this was our mother's rule), and we always let them go eventually.

In the mountains, the animals made the rules. Rattlesnakes

received a lot of distance and respect. Squirrels and chipmunks could be enticed with pieces of cookie, but never came within reach. We once discovered a small cave and crawled in, only to encounter a pair of glowing eyes in the darkness. We left without waiting for an introduction.

We never tried to bring wild animals home as pets. Our house was already filled with an assortment of cats, dogs, birds, rabbits, hamsters, fish, gerbils, and guinea pigs.

Our most vivid lesson in living with nature's creatures came after we found the submarine.

We never knew what its real function was, but we discovered it in a field one winter: a metal cylinder about six feet long and three feet high. It had two round holes in the top, just big enough for a child to slip through, and it made a perfect submarine.

We climbed in and headed for the ocean, and when an occasional curious horse approached to give us a sniff, he was promptly torpedoed.

We spent a lot of time that winter protecting the fields from enemy battleships and wrestling with giant squid. Then spring brought other interests, and the submarine was forgotten for a while. In the late summer we recalled our submarine adventures and headed for the field to resume sea duty. The submarine gleamed silently in the tall grass. My brother climbed inside and I quickly followed. I soon found myself surrounded by thousands of wasps.

I remember that, for a brief instant, I was tempted to study their activities. What a chance to gain personal insight into life in a wasps' nest! But within a couple of seconds the shock wore off and panic took over. Although my brother had headed for the exit first, I nearly beat him out the hole. It was a tight fit

with two of us squeezing through together, but all the screaming probably helped.

We scrambled out the hole and took off, practically leaping
the fences in our path. And we didn't stop running until we
slammed the door securely from inside our house.

After a while I calmed down enough to realize I hadn't
been stung at all. We don't know if they even followed us. We
never turned around to look.

While the experience didn't leave me with a desire to form
closer friendships with wasps, it did give me something to
think about. How could I have dropped into a wasps' nest uninvited and escaped unscathed? Maybe they just thought we
were two of the biggest, funniest-looking wasps they'd ever
seen. After all, why else would we be dropping in uninvited?

Or maybe they were just too busy playing submarine.

from CHRISTIAN SCIENCE MONITOR

Mockingbird Summer

LARRY HABEGGER

I came home one evening this spring to the rollicking song of a mockingbird in the trees outside my house. The song filled an empty space in me I'd forgotten existed, because it was the voice of a long lost friend I thought I'd never hear again. But he was finally back, or one of his progeny was here in his place, singing the same song that had filled my nights with inexpressible joy just a few years before.

It was a time I've come to call my mockingbird summer, a unique period in my hillside neighborhood in San Francisco. We'd always had mockingbirds here, but this one was something else. His song began late one spring afternoon and continued into the evening, just outside my window, through the dinner hour and on into the night. I opened my window wide before bed and stuck my head out into the darkness. That mockingbird just sang and sang, up and down the scale, sounding like a cat, then a squirrel, a chattering chipmunk, a warbler, a jay, an oriole. His repertoire was boundless and he continued singing as I drifted off to sleep. His music lightened my dreams and he was still at it, or at it again, when I awoke at dawn.

It was a virtuoso performance, one not to be repeated there or anywhere else, I thought, but that evening he started up again and continued his song well into the night just as before. After several consecutive nights of this irrepressible song I began to expect it, and indeed all summer it went on, every night, all night. He was singing as if this was all he was ever meant to do, as if his entire reason for being was wrapped up in his singing through the night, spreading joy into the dark, silent world.

That "nightingale" outside my window reminded me how much pleasure birds had given me throughout my life. When I was a boy of nine or ten I spent many thrilling mornings rising at dawn, grabbing my father's binoculars, and racing off to the woods surrounding a marshy lake about a half mile from home. Etched in my memory are images of those pink mornings when the world was a-chatter, the shrubs busy with wrens and juncos, the trees alive with woodpeckers and thrushes and robins, the lake swarming with mallards and coots, and terns swooping above.

I can still see the sunny morning in a nearby park when I lay on my belly, propped on elbows, binoculars trained on a flicker hammering an oak tree so close the bird filled the entire frame, his colors radiant in the sunshine. I can see the black and white flash of a red-headed woodpecker flying from tree to tree. I can hear the morning call of a meadowlark on a wooden fence, see the black V on the yellow breast as brilliant as it appeared in my Peterson field guide. I remember dusty ballfields where I saw small, unremarkable birds that on closer inspection had two tiny rabbit ears, a feature that seemed so exotic I couldn't believe what I was seeing. Peterson showed that they were horned larks, a species I didn't know existed and wouldn't have believed if I had.

In those childhood years birds took me into the woods, out to the meadows, onto the margins of lakes and swamps. By

drawing me into the outdoors they gave me a precious gift—
an appreciation of nature—and drew from me a certain kind
of love. Love for them, for their surroundings, for the wide
world they and I inhabited.

from THE GIFT OF BIRDS

Memories With Mitzy

KATHRYN LAY

$\mathcal{M}$itzy followed me around the yard like a dog. Her pink ears turned as I called her name. Hide-and-seek was our favorite game. Her twitching rabbit nose always seemed to be able to find my hiding places. I'd fall backwards laughing as she thumped her large hind feet, as if to tell me, "Found you again!" Then she'd crawl onto my chest and nibble at my hair.

My best friend, Belinda, had suddenly started hanging around with another classmate, and I was left out. With young girls, three is almost always a crowd. My young heart was broken, so I spent more time than ever with Mitzy. She couldn't shop with me at the mall, ride bikes with me, or play board games, but she would always be my friend.

"You've got a phone call," Mom shouted one Saturday afternoon. I scratched behind Mitzy's ears and ran inside.

"It's Belinda," Mom said.

My stomach jumped. Belinda! She missed me, I bet. She and Teresa probably had a fight and Belinda wanted to apologize to me.

I grabbed the phone. "Belinda? Guess what Mitzy just did, it was so cute. . . . "

"Um, yeah . . . but I need to ask you something. Can I have my necklace back?"

I squeezed the phone. "The one with the shells on it?"

"Yeah."

The tears came and I shrugged. I knew she couldn't see my shrug, but I couldn't talk for a moment. I had borrowed the necklace a few months ago and Belinda said I could keep it because we were friends forever, and she'd know where it was if she ever wanted to wear it.

"Are you wearing it somewhere special?" I asked.

Belinda was quiet a moment. "Teresa wants to wear it when we go to my family's beach party."

I really felt sick then. Mitzy and I had always gone with Belinda to the beach party. Her youngest cousin loved Mitzy and always brought carrot sticks for her.

"Oh," I said. "I guess you can come get it now."

After I hung up, I ran outside and buried my face in Mitzy's soft fur.

Belinda rode her bike over and came into the backyard. She stroked Mitzy's back. "How's Mitzy doing?"

"Fine," I said. As if she cared.

"Did she ever learn to fetch?"

I shook my head. "No, she just follows me. If I throw a carrot stick, she'll go chew on it. But she doesn't bring it back."

Belinda laughed. "Told you she isn't a dog. But it sure was funny the way you taught her to beg."

Suddenly we were petting Mitzy and telling stories of the fun things the three of us had done together. Belinda had helped me choose Mitzy from all the other bunnies. She helped me pick Mitzy's name. And Mitzy had made Belinda laugh when she was worried about her dad in the hospital.

"Um, do you think it's too late to ask your parents about the beach party?" Belinda asked.

I grinned. "No, I'll go ask now." I stood up, then said, "Do you think Teresa will like Mitzy?"

"Of course. Besides, she's got one of those flop-eared bunnies. I bet Pepper and Mitzy could be friends."

Mitzy hopped around us, her fluffy tail standing straight up. "Yeah, I bet we could all be friends," I said.

Mitzy was my best friend, though. I could never thank her for all the memories she'd given Belinda and me. Now we were about to start some new ones.

Stop the Car

MONICA WOOD

$\mathcal{M}$y best friend Robin and I like gear. We're bird watch-ers—"birders" to those in the know—and our bird paraphernalia makes us feel lucky. We have vests with 24 pockets. We have field guide holders and notebooks that hook to belt loops. We have bird whistles and gum boots and other needful things. Birding is a hobby that requires long, Zenlike stretches of patience. The right accoutrements—an extra spotting scope, say, or a bag of chocolate bismarcks—can turn a drizzly vigil into a festival of anticipation. Gear is good.

On this wintry Maine day, however, we're carrying a bit more gear than we bargained for: Anna and Kate, Robin's children. Anna is seven months old and oblivious, but Kate, at two and a half, is well acquainted with the art of expectation. "Where's Kate's owl?" she asks every hundred feet or so, her shoes ticking against the plastic ridge of her car seat. The owl in question is the great gray, a rare, magnificent winter visitor that Robin and I have firmly resolved to witness, babysitter or no babysitter.

During the ride, a straight shot north on Route 1 that passes frozen inlets and craggy little fishing towns (in short, all the places where there is absolutely no chance of spotting a great gray owl), the kids are perfect. Pink-cheeked and snoring, these polished little apples of our eyes have fallen asleep. Robin and I chat softly, wondering how a great gray owl might look in person. I read aloud the owl's description from the old Peterson's, the new Peterson's, the Audubon, and the National Geographic field guides. We eat a couple of chocolate bismarcks for luck.

An hour later we approach a spit of land that juts like a broken finger into the Atlantic Ocean. Robin slows down as I read the directions, and we find an ordinary country road flanked by peeling houses and fallow fields. "Start looking," I whisper, and Kate startles awake. I try a preemptive strike, lest she wake the baby. "Hi, sweetie," I croon, handing her a doughnut—backup gear that does the trick. This is Kate's first doughnut, and she is pleased. We are geniuses. We are birders extraordinaire.

We inch down the road until we spot three other gear-laden birders gathered at the edge of a field. Within seconds Robin and I are out of the car. We sidle over to these people and ask, "Is he here?"

There are two kinds of birders in this world. We are the kind who hug and dance. They are the other kind. We manage to extract the relevant information: the owl has been seen in this very field at more or less this very time for three days running. That's the good news. The bad news is that Kate's doughnut is gone. The sound emanating from Robin's car, reminiscent of screech owls I once heard in the north Maine woods, alerts us that we're about three minutes to meltdown. We retreat to the car, trying to appease the spoilsports in the backseat. One of the birders knocks tersely on the window: "Maybe if you drive around for a while they'll fall asleep." Mortified by this helpful advice, Robin starts the car. As we leave the scene, harboring just the tiniest wish to leave the kids in a snowbank—not forever, just for ten minutes, even five, long enough for us to catch the smallest glimpse—Anna falls back to sleep. It's a miracle! But Kate is not so easily duped; our adventure is cut short. "That's that," Robin sighs. "Let's go home."

A minute later, at the far end of the road near a saggy ranch house, I feel my mouth drop open. "Stop the car!" I shout. Robin stops. Kate stops. "Look," I tell them, pointing to the wintry scrub of yard. There, staring out from the naked branches of a birch, stands the great gray owl. It turns its head to leer at us with fire-yellow eyes.

We bound out of the car, pulling Kate with us and leaving all our gear, for the owl is so close—ten feet at most—that we can see the delicate parentheses of feathers that frame its massive head. We gape at the owl. We name him Frank. We hug and dance. Kate stands between us, looking up. Then, as if delivering a message only owls can comprehend, she opens her mouth and screams. Wings lifting like a velvet cape, the owl disconnects its heavy body from the spindly tree that held him.

Oh, what a day! On the way home we ponder what propels some birds to wander thousands of miles from home and other mysteries of the natural world. After a while, it strikes me: we could still be waiting in vain at the edge of that empty field. I glance into the backseat at the gear jumbled up with diapers and size one mittens. We didn't need the binoculars. We didn't need the scope. We sure didn't need a bird whistle. What we needed, as it turns out, was the kids.

from THE GIFT OF BIRDS

A Tale of Two Kitties

JUNE TORENCE

They say that cats have nine lives. Well, I don't know about that. But I do know one cat who had two lives. His name was Smokey; at least that's what I called him. He was a gray-striped tom with a pink nose, four white paws, and a silky-furred right ear that folded over at the tip. I found him shivering in our garage as a kitten when I was nine years old and kept him hidden in my bedroom for a week until I was sure my mom would let me keep him. A stranger might not have thought he was much to look at, but to me he was the cutest kitten in the world. My mother used to joke about how I was the only girl in Indian Hills, Colorado, who'd fall in love with a "dog-eared" cat.

By the time I was 11, Smokey had pretty much established his own daily routine of running out and about in the daytime, always returning home in time for dinner, after which he'd curl up on my bed. When I'd slip beneath the covers for the night, he'd move close to my face, nudge his head right under my chin, and purr like a warm, small-appliance motor. I never had a bad dream when Smokey slept beside me. He liked my three brothers, but it was obvious that he was a one-kid cat. And I was his girl. Or so I thought.

One night that July, Smokey didn't come home. I was upset, but my mother assured me it wasn't unusual for a cat to wander off for an adventure now and then. I spent the next few days searching for him, calling his name and expecting any minute to see him, but there was no sign of him. By the end of the week, we were all upset.

My mother agreed that I should go to the general store and put up a "Missing" notice with Smokey's picture. I picked out one where he was lying sphinxlike across my pillow; his bent ear and white paws clearly visible. When I wrote down his coloring and distinguishing marks, it was hard to keep from crying.

My brother Dave went with me to the store to post the notice for Smokey. Once it was up, we stood back to see if it was in a good spot. Well, it was in a good spot, all right. It was right next to a notice for another missing cat, "Ranger"—and the only difference between them was their names. Their descriptions were identical.

I wrote down the phone number and called the moment we got home. The girl who answered said that her missing cat, Ranger, always stayed out at night and came home in the morning but hadn't shown up in a week. I told her that my cat, Smokey—same coloring, same bent right ear—went out in the morning and came home in the evening and that he hadn't shown up in a week. It was a little too much of a coincidence to be a coincidence. With an unspoken twinge of betrayal, we both conceded that her Ranger and my Smokey were one and the same cat—and that he had been living a double life! So much for a one-kid cat. But two-timing tom or not, both of us loved him, and he was still missing.

The girl's name was Evelyn Boldoven, and we arranged to meet the following day. She was a year older than I, which was probably why we hadn't known each other even though she lived just a quarter of a mile away. She brought over her pictures of Ranger, and I brought out my pictures of Smokey. We spent the afternoon sharing stories about "our dog-eared, one-kid cat," alternately sniffling and laughing at the similarity of his two-household antics. By dinnertime we'd gone through more than half a box of Kleenex and had become best friends.

Evelyn and I handmade flyers for our missing cat ("answers to the name of Smokey or Ranger"), passed them out all around town, and kept each other from giving up hope by recounting amazing stories of lost animals who'd miraculously found their way home after years. But by the end of August, even these took on a hollow ring.

Then, a week before school started, we got a phone call that seemed too good to be true. It was from a woman in Golden, a town about 10 miles away, saying she'd seen our flyer in a gas station and believed she had our cat. Her son had found it about a month ago on the side of the road, bloody and near death from an animal attack, and she'd been nursing it back to health. She said that she'd named him "Marker" because of his bent ear.

My mother drove Evelyn and me to Golden that same afternoon, cautioning us not to get too excited in case the cat wasn't ours. How many dog-eared cats could there be? We wondered but really didn't want to know. Holding hands and squeezing tightly, we followed the woman into the house where she said Marker was resting. But the moment we saw him there was no doubt that Marker wasn't Marker. He was Smokey. He was Ranger. He was ours, and he was alive! His nonstop purring all the way home told us that he was as happy to be found as we were to find him.

Smokey/Ranger continued to live his two lives—dividing

his days and nights and love between Evelyn's house and ours—until advancing age and illness curtailed him. When his health worsened, we knew the kindest thing to do was to set him free from his suffering. Evelyn and I were with him when he died. He seemed to know we were both there—stroking his white paws, caressing his bent ear—and he drifted from us peacefully, purring to the end.

No, Smokey wasn't the one-kid cat I once thought he was. He was just the best cat that ever was.

from HEART SONGS FOR ANIMAL LOVERS

P.S. Evelyn, who's remained my best friend for all these years, says the same thing about Ranger.

Peco's Run

CATHERINE E. LORD

When I was a little girl I lived in Evansville, Indiana, down at the southern tip of the state where the Ohio River ran wide and muddy, on a tree-lined road called Spring Street. It was appropriately named, as I was in the springtime of my life and the seasons shaped my memories.

In the spring I eagerly awaited the sudden reappearance of crocuses by the small steps which connected the driveway to a short cement sidewalk leading to my front door. Their blue and yellow smiles heralded the coming of fresh, pale green leaves on the maple trees in the front yard, followed soon after by the strongly perfumed flowers of the tulip poplar stretching joyfully in the backyard behind the kitchen window.

Summertime brought the slap of a rope across the poplar's lowest branch, a rope which would be pegged into the rich, dark soil at a sharp angle. An old blue tarp straddled the line, and the tent of adventures came to life.

The maples out front offered dappled shade for childhood games, but gently sacrificed their leaves in autumn. Their warm, musty scent surrounded me in the crisp air as I raked "lanes" and "avenues," creating city blocks in the golden brown carpet. In return we gave the maples our childish laughter as we jumped gleefully into the crackling leaf mounds.

My woody friends rested in winter, only occasionally giving a little shake of a powder-laden branch to join in our snowball fights. Colored water spouted from former dish detergent bottles, magically creating words and images in the pristine snow. Snacks and drinks left too long in snow forts froze solid, but a hearty pioneer would eat what he or she had stored.

The Spring Street seasons held special moments for me, a blessed human child. However, I doubted they spared any of their splendor for poor Peco. Time would prove my supposition wrong, but gift me with important lessons in the process.

Peco (pronounced PEE-ko) appeared one day in a fenced pen next door, between the neighbor's house and ours. A large, heavy-coated, black-and-white dog, he was the first Alaskan Husky I'd ever seen. From my youthful vantage point, peering between brick-red painted slats of wood, he seemed enormous. My parents later informed me that our neighbors' son had recently moved back to our area and would be living with his parents for awhile. Peco had moved in, too.

I never saw Peco leave his enclosure. The son may have taken him out at times, but I was never privy to his release. Day after day, season after season, poor Peco paced the span of his cell, or sprawled on the concrete in apparent acceptance of his fate.

A few times during the green and shady summer, I was allowed to traverse his boundary in order to brush the dense black-and-white coat. I remember being surprised at how thick his fur was, and amazed by the large and numerous clumps of soft hair appearing in my hand or the brush. It seemed as if there was to be no end to my task. For my efforts I was paid a dime. Peco, for his part, lay panting quietly throughout the ordeal in a patch of shade next to the house. The dime lay cold and small in my hand, but Peco looked into my eyes with what I can only deem gratitude.

Lesson Number One: The joy from giving comfort to one who cannot help himself is beyond price.

Summer passed into autumn, and autumn in its turn lay down for winter. Peco paced off the days in his cell.

Snow eventually blanketed Spring Street. Short, snow-suited figures with bread sacks rubber-banded over their mittened hands appeared, to be joined later by other little people. Round, misshapen people, with lumps of charcoal for eyes, mouths and buttons, carrots for noses, sticks or twigs for arms, and (if they were lucky) bright fluffy scarves to keep them warm. A holiday mood entered our neighborhood, quietly injecting its magic into each living thing.

Then it happened.

One day it started to snow again. But this was no ordinary snow. No, this was a *magic* snow. It came pouring from the skies, heavier and heavier, until midday was darkened and individual flakes disappeared. This snow was that special snow, thick and powdery, but moist enough to hold a good shape when packed. Snow that we children couldn't wait to play in.

Finally the white deluge slowed its pace, and throughout the neighborhood the little people were zipped into their snowsuits. Knees were lifted high in order to break a trail through that winter wonderland. Then a shout ripped through the icy air.

"Peco's loose!"

A bear, a wolf, a heaving black beast raced through the deep snow! Grinning from ear to ear, tongue waving teasingly from the side of his mouth, Peco exulted in his escape. His plumed tail waved like a victor's flag over his haunches. Scaling a six-foot fence was nothing to this valiant knight. He barked loudly, joyfully, inviting us all to join in his celebration.

We gave chase. Slipping, sliding, we lurched at him, only to find ourselves grasping empty air. He sprinted through the front yards of Spring Street, up one side and back down the other. In, out and around us he danced, weaving a tapestry of pure, unadulterated delight.

He charged toward me and I saw my chance. Tensing my legs beneath me, I bent my knees then leaped through the air, fingers outspread, reaching, grabbing, slipping . . . gripping him by the collar!

"I've got him!" I shouted, high on the excitement of the hunt.

Peco didn't agree. Or maybe he didn't understand English. Regardless, I found myself being dragged through the drifts on my right side. My weight barely slowed him down. Peco reveled in the game. This was what he had been bred for, born for: pulling people through the snow. Exultant, every muscle in his body smoothly striving to accomplish the job at hand, his eyes seemed to shout, "Yes! Yes! This is what I was meant to do! This is who I am!"

My ride lasted only a few short yards before I lost my grip and fell, although it seemed much longer. Peco bounded away. Spitting snow out of my mouth, the excitement drained away as I lay panting, feeling the ache in my arms and defeat in my spirit. Someone else would get the glory of capturing this magnificent creature. Yet I hoped his charge would not end too soon.

Who could have guessed that such a being existed on the other side of the brick-red fence? I had supposed that Peco had resigned himself to his prison, and perhaps for a time he forgot that he was an Alaskan Husky. Forgot during the long months of imprisonment, in the heat and the rain and the monotony, that he had been created for a purpose. All it took was one special snow, however, and his memory came flooding back. And that memory caused him to dance and shout for joy.

That was the Second Lesson: Though we may reach a point in life when all seems dark, and our spirits have withered to nothing more than a distant memory, all it takes is a special moment to remind us who we are, that we are still our essential selves, born for a purpose. Imprisoned for a time perhaps, but with the potential to break free in the proper season, and once again dance and shout for joy.

Misty, the Kid Magnet

CAROL FLEISCHMAN

$\mathcal{A}$lthough I'm not a mother, children are an important part of my life. Eight years ago, I went to The Seeing Eye in New Jersey for my first guide dog, Misty. Since then, I learned that all the inquisitive kids we met would be a welcome addition to our lives (one we couldn't avoid, anyway).

One day, my husband, Don, Misty and I walked through a holiday festival where there were one hundred decorated trees. We wove our way through the crowd while my husband described each ornament and display to me. Misty received as many cheerful compliments as those decorations.

"You're SO COOL."

"Awesome dog!"

"What pretty eyes!" and "Look at those huge teeth!"

Misty enjoyed all the praise as her plumed tail slapped against my body. When it was time to leave, we followed Don's directions, snaking our way toward a wall of glass doors. Don pulled the handle and a rush of cold hit my face—*Brrr!* My husband swung around to look at me, and saw that a featherweight toddler, who got out of his parent's sight, had joined our parade. Draped over Misty as she walked out of the hall, the child almost rode out the door. Within seconds, his frantic mother rushed over and scooped him into her arms, despite his protest, "Doggie, doggie, mine!"

Misty and I cannot stroll through the neighborhood, go into a restaurant, or visit the mall without being surrounded by small voices asking big questions like, "Does your dog know when to cross at stop lights?"

"No, dogs are color blind. I listen for the cars and when it's safe to go, I give Misty commands like *forward, right,* or *left* at street crossings. Then, she looks for my matching hand signal and pulls me in the direction we want to go."

Sometimes we're pressed for time, but I've always got a minute to answer their concerns. I hear the worry in their voices, asking "Why is there a dog in this store?" and "Will your dog protect you if a robber tries to hurt you?" For me, there is no such thing as running into a store and getting out fast. Even if Don leaves us to search for an item, when he returns Misty and I are circled by a pint-sized audience. This is my chance to teach kids how Misty has given me independence and dignity once again.

Speaking at schools and libraries about my life with my guide dog has become popular. All my nieces, nephews, and godchildren have a unique "show and tell" claim on their blind aunt and her dog partner. One of them demonstrates a promising career as our agent because she introduces us in her classroom as "The Carol and Misty Show."

I'm never sure who gets more out of our talks, the kids or me. The question-and-answer sessions at the end are full of energy, and are usually followed by enthusiastic thank-you notes:

"I wish I could be a dog like Misty."

"I was a puppy raiser, and my pup is with a blind man. I hope King's as happy as your dog."

"You and Misty make blindness seem like fun, but it's not."

Each time I meet new friends, there's an opportunity to make a home run. Richard, a boy in my neighborhood, is one of my devoted fans. In fact, I recommend his uplifting words for every middle-aged woman. When he sees me, his unique greeting stays with me for a long time. "Hi, Seeing Eye Girl. When are you coming back to my school?" I haven't been called a girl in twenty years, and that puts a bounce in my step.

A Real Star

LOIS DROEGE AND PAM HARDEN

Mike and his dad stood near the pasture gate watching his young colt eat grass. Mike laughed. "Look at him, Dad. He has all that grass in front of him, but now he wants what's on the other side of the fence. Why do horses do that? Are they dumb?"

"They may be smarter than you think, Mike. It looks to me as if the grass on the other side is greener. Actually, horses can be taught to do many things, so they aren't dumb at all. Just think of the ones in the circus who bow, stand up, walk on their back legs, and do many other tricks."

"Do you think I could teach Star any tricks?" Mike asked.

"Now, I don't know if Star could do the things circus horses do, but perhaps you could teach him something else." Dad started back to the barn. "He's your colt, so why don't you give it a try?" he called.

That night Mike talked to his mom. "I'm trying to think of something I could teach Star to do that is different from just bowing or things like that. Can you think of anything?"

"How about teaching him to ride you on his back?"

"Oh, Mom, you know we'll teach him that when he's older. I mean something now. I'd like my friends to see how smart he is."

"I'm sure you'll think of something, but right now it's bed-time, and you have school tomorrow."

Mike went to sleep that night thinking about Star. In his dream, Star became a famous horse, and by morning, Mike was convinced that he would have no trouble teaching his colt a trick or two.

That afternoon he rushed home after school and took Star out of his stall and into the pasture. He soon found out that Star would not stand still for one minute to be taught anything. He would break away from him, kick up his heels, and circle the pasture at breakneck speed. By the time Mike caught him, he was too exhausted to hold him for more than a second. He finally gave up and, disappointed, walked back toward the house. It looked as though Star was just not smart enough to learn.

Noticing his tether ball, he picked it up. Mike decided to at-tach it to its pole and knock it around to get rid of his frustration.

Star, standing near the fence, whinnied at him and curled his lip. He looked so funny that Mike had to laugh. Just to see what Star would do, he threw the ball to him. Star nosed the ball, playfully knocked it away, then ran up close. He picked it up by the hook and took off with it in his mouth.

Mike could hardly believe what he saw. He chased after Star. When he dropped the ball, Mike threw it back to him. The colt picked the ball up and circled the pasture with it in his mouth. Mike clapped his hands. "Bring it here, Star. Bring it here!"

Star had stopped at the far end of the pasture with the ball in his mouth. Suddenly he ran at full speed to the fence and dropped the ball at Mike's feet.

"You did it! You did it! I can't believe it!" Mike shouted. "Mom," he called, "watch Star!"

Again he threw the ball into the pasture. Star started after it. When Mike called him to bring it back, he came running. He dropped the ball near the fence in front of Mike, then took off, kicking up his heels, as if he knew he had done something remarkable.

By now, Mike's mother had reached the fence. "I can't believe what I'm seeing!" she said. "Did he really do that?"

"Watch now," Mike answered as he threw the ball back into the field. This time Star ran up to the ball and kicked it for several yards before he picked it up in his mouth and ran with it. "Do you believe it, Mom? He can actually play ball with me!"

Star was galloping around the pasture with the ball in his mouth when Mike noticed that cars were pulling off the highway to watch the unusual sight. Mike almost burst with pride when several people got out of their cars and walked to the fence. One man said, "I've never seen a horse do that before. Did you teach him?"

"Not really, sir, the colt actually taught me!"

"Gosh, he must be super smart," the man said.

"He sure is!" Mike replied. "I guess he's just about the smartest colt around."

The man laughed. "Well, I don't know about that, but he certainly is the star of this show!"

"I guess I gave him the right name because it looks as though he is going to be the star of the whole neighborhood."

from BOYS' QUEST

Chicken Dreams Can Come True

RENIE SZILAK BURGHARDT

When my family and I escaped our communist, Soviet-occupied country, Hungary, we landed in a refugee camp in Austria. The year was 1947, and our future looked bleak. But children can find hope even in the most hopeless situations, and this was certainly true of me.

DP Camp Spittal was on the outskirts of the town of Spittal. It consisted of old army barracks, lined up like soldiers, as far as the eyes could see, and inside the barracks the walls were made of cardboard. There was a common kitchen where everyone went for their meals. There were two churches. There were barracks serving as shower and bathroom facilities. And we had our own school. I spent four years at Camp Spittal, growing from child to a young teenager.

However, Camp Spittal was surrounded by another world, a beautiful natural world of mountains, clear cold streams, rolling flower-carpeted hills, and small farms dotted with grazing animals. It was this other world that ignited my imagination with its beauty and filled my heart with hope.

My best friend, Lenka, and I slipped away from the dismal, crowded world of the camp as often as we could. We roamed the hills and valleys, explored and grew to love nature, and shared our hopes and dreams while filling our stomachs with wild blueberries or other of nature's offerings.

"Someday, I am going to live in the country, in a house among large, shady trees," I would tell Lenka dreamily. "And I'll have many animals around, too."

One day, our ramble took us to a farm nestled at the bottom of a pine-covered hill. The farmhouse was alpine in style, and in the neat, flower-filled yard, a woman in a dirndl frock was tossing feed to a flock of white bantam chickens.

"Oh, look! Aren't they adorable?" I said excitedly to Lenka. Animals, whether two- or four-legged, were my passion.

"So you like my little chickens, eh?" the woman said, overhearing me. "Why don't you open the gate and come and take a closer look."

We ventured into the yard and introduced ourselves. I sat down in the grass and made little chicken noises at the small bantams. Soon, a hen and rooster jumped right into my lap and began pecking at the buttons on my shirt. The woman, who told us to call her Gerda, then treated us to generous slices of cherry strudel and tall glasses of fresh milk.

When we were ready to leave, she had a surprise for me. "Since that hen and rooster seem to have taken to you, I decided to let you keep them," she said, setting the pair into a small crate. I was ecstatic!

"But you don't have a place to keep chickens," Lenka reminded me on the way home.

"I'll just leave them in the crate tonight. Tomorrow, I'll figure out something else," I replied, my heart filling with the joy of this new ownership. I decided to call the pair Hansel and Gretel.

When I walked into our tiny cubicle in the barrack, my grandfather took one look at my bantams and bellowed, "You can NOT keep chickens in the barrack!"

"But why not? They are tiny, and I'll keep them with me wherever I go," I said, trying to be convincing. "They won't be any trouble at all."

"It's summer now, so there is no school. But what about in the fall when school begins again?" my grandmother asked.

"I don't know. But I'll figure something out by that time," I quickly answered.

"There is nothing to figure out. You cannot keep chickens here. It is too late now, but tomorrow morning you will return them to where they came from," Grandfather ordered sternly. And that was that.

Later that night, as I lay in my cot in the barrack, the pungent odor of chicken litter began drifting up to my nose. I covered my face with my blanket, but I was still determined to find a way to keep the diminutive pair. However, at 4:30 that morning, something happened. Something that finally made me concede. Hansel began to crow! He crowed with all the shrill might of a bantam rooster! Grandfather jumped out of bed with a thud. "What the . . . ," I heard him grumble sleepily, while I held on to Hansel as hard as I could, for I knew his neck was in grave danger!

Meanwhile, a pajama-clad crowd began gathering outside our cubicle, and they didn't sound very happy. Grandfather went out and apologized profusely, promising it would not happen again. The grumbling crowd shuffled back to bed. I dressed and quickly took the crate outside and waited for daylight, while tears streamed down my face.

Hansel and Gretel were returned to the farm, early. When I

explained to Gerda what had happened, she laughed so hard that tears rolled down her rosy cheeks. Finally she said, sympathetically, "I tell you what—I will keep them here, but you can come and see them anytime you like."

And that's just what I did. Hansel and Gretel always seemed happy to see me, too, coming to me as soon as they saw me, comforting me with their little clucking noises, as if to say, "We still love you. We understand."

By the following spring, we received the news we had been hoping for. We had been accepted to immigrate to the United States of America! I hurried to the farm to tell Gerda. "I have heard that everyone has the chance to realize their dream in America," I told her. "That means that one day I will live in the country, and then I can raise all the bantam chickens that I want."

It took over 30 years for that young refugee girl to realize her dream. But in 1983, I finally moved to the country. Now, I live in a rustic house shaded by massive oaks and hickories. And in the yard, the happy scratching of my fuzzy white, orange and brown silkie bantams reminds me daily that, in America, chicken dreams can come true!

LESSONS WE REMEMBER

"Teach me to be more like you,
old, gentle beast.
As wise as any I've ever known."

SANTI MEUNIER

*A*nimals are good teachers. Without a word, they explain what love is. Without a reprimand they let us know when we've done something wrong, and then they show us what forgiveness is. In the simplest possible ways they demonstrate loyalty, devotion and generosity. And, most important, they help us to understand how much God cares about us.

A Simple Prayer

KATHRYN LAY

"*P*lease let me see a frog tonight. In Jesus' name. Amen."

I hugged my four-year-old daughter good-night and tucked her into bed with her favorite book. Her prayer was simple and cute, something from a book of kids' prayers. We had been talking about frogs and lizards and turtles that day, three of her favorite creatures.

"When will the frog come?" Michelle asked.

I smiled. "Well, sweetheart, I haven't seen any frogs around here this year. We'll just have to wait and see."

I felt bad, knowing that she would be disappointed.

"God can do anything," she announced. "Just like my Daddy."

A lump filled my throat. She trusted her father and her heavenly Father. Recent difficult times had made me doubt God's love for me. I didn't want her having those same doubts.

I went into the kitchen to do the dishes. With hands sunk in hot, soapy water, I closed my eyes. "I know it's a silly request, God, to see a frog late at night. But there's something about the way she truly believes you'll answer her prayer. Do you hear her? Do you hear me?"

My husband returned home late from a meeting at church.

Michelle had been asleep an hour. Richard and I talked over our day, sitting down to relax and catch up together.

"Oops, laundry!" I said, jumping up to move the wet clothes from the washer to the dryer. I turned on the garage light, startled by movement near the open door that led to the backyard.

Tippy, our terrier, barked at the corner, stopping to sniff at something. I took a careful step forward, ready to run if one of our giant, fast-moving waterbugs should suddenly head my way.

Near the back door sat a large, bug-eyed, brown frog.

"Outside," I ordered the dog. After a momentary chase, with the frog being two hops ahead, I held the bulging, squirming creature in my hands and carried my prize into the house.

"Hey, look," I said, holding it out to my husband. "I think Tippy was about to have a late-night frog snack."

"Wow, it's too bad Michelle's not awake," my husband said offhandedly.

Suddenly I remembered her prayer. "Quick!" I said. "Let's wake her up!"

My surprised husband stared at me as if I'd done one too many loads of laundry. Under most circumstances, after a long day with our active child, and an even longer evening of convincing her to go to bed, I rarely encouraged awakening of our little sleeping beauty.

But this was different.

"She needs to see this frog," I explained.

My heart raced as I forced myself to wake her up gently. A heavy sleeper, she was slow to open her eyes.

"What, Mommy?"

"Look!" I proudly placed the frog in her hands. She held it

and petted it, more sleepy than interested, and not the least bit surprised that her prayer had been answered.

But I was overwhelmed at the quick response to her simple and faith-filled prayer. What a loving Father, to see how important a small child's request was, giving a chance for her to see his power.

My faith took a leap that night as I set the frog free in our front yard. He blinked wide eyes at me and seemed to watch me a moment before he hopped away.

Sometimes, my daughter teaches me more than I teach her. And sometimes, a frog isn't a prince, it's an angel.

Friday:
A Mother's Story

BETTY FORBIS

One day, long ago, I was visiting my aunt in Albany, New York. I heard a dog barking insistently and looked out the window and saw a young, enthusiastic ball of energy tied with a rope, about eighteen inches long, to a picnic table. He seemed to be calling out to anyone who would listen, "It's a beautiful day. Is anyone there who will explore the world with me?" I asked my aunt about the dog, and she told me his story. She had often called the humane society because the dog was tied to a short rope all day until his owners would take him in at night directly to the basement. Occasionally, his enthusiasm would allow him to break loose to explore life, and the owners would chase him, throwing rocks at him, to get him back to the picnic table. At that moment, I knew I had to have that dog.

I asked Aunt Virginia to go with me to talk to the owners. I had no idea what I was going to say. When the woman came to the door I heard myself making up a story that my young children were desolate because we had to put our dog to sleep and that their dog looked just like the dog we missed so terribly. Did this woman know if there were any others that looked like their dog? She told me her children had given the dog to her and her husband. They were thinking of getting rid of it. I was shocked, and told her I would be returning home to Massachusetts and would be grateful if I could take the dog with me.

In a half hour she brought the dog to me. He seemed to know that he was starting a new life. He never looked back toward his owners. This beautiful, cream-colored dog of uncertain origin was entrusting his life to me. He was about the size of a German shepherd. We speculated about his origin and thought he was a mix of Lab and husky. He had never been inside a house before and was bouncing from couch to chair to table and landed on my lap wetting me with kisses saying, "Thank you, thank you. . . . Now, let's go, let's see the world!"

As he settled in next to me on the front seat, with his head on my lap, I said to him, "Your life will never be the same." And it wasn't. Neither was ours. We drove home to Massachusetts, and he seemed to know that he had to be patient for three hours. When we pulled into the driveway he jumped up to get his first glimpse of his new world. He saw a big yard with a stake in the ground attached to a very, very long rope and a run in the backyard that faced onto a large wooded area. He saw three of my four grown children, a black Lab, and a black Norwegian forest cat . . . and he knew that, yes, his life would never be the same! Much excitement followed. He cajoled the Lab, queen of the house and suspect of this young, rambunctious intruder, to play with him. He treed the cat much to his own amazement. "How did I do that?" He ran around, jumping and laughing with us all. Friends came to welcome him to this new world. Occasionally, he would stop, lean against one of us, and cover us with kisses.

What would we name this new member of the family? It was on Friday that he was rescued and on Friday that a new way of life for all of us started. So, it was decided, "Friday" was his name.

When we finally went inside, we discovered he had this incredible ability to jump straight up into the air! If there was something in his path like a coffee table, his exuberance drove him to the most direct route: He would jump straight up over it! If someone was sitting with their legs stretched out, he would jump straight up into the air and over; he was like a kangaroo! We played this game for years and years.

The first morning in his new home, I awoke and went to look for him. I came into the living room and he was sitting on a high table looking out the window. He had never been in a house, he didn't know about furniture. He learned many things in the days that followed. In a short time he learned that it was okay to go downstairs. He wouldn't be locked away, alone in a basement. He was free to come and go. He also learned that a raised hand to his head was no cause to cringe . . . it was a loving touch. Friday and my son Scott formed that special bond between man and dog. Scott spent hours training him to voice commands and to walk with a leash for his own safety. Loyalty and love worked both ways. My belief about loyalty and love is that the more you give, the more you get. I don't know who loved more or who was more loyal, but they both gave all they had and received beyond expectations. Rain, snow, sleet, cold, warm sunshine, day or night, Scott would take Friday to fulfill his dream of exploring life and the world.

He ran free in the woods chasing every movement and every scent. There were deer for him to chase: "Don't run away, I just want to play!" There were squirrels, raccoons, rabbits, and strange rustlings in the underbrush. Such an athlete! Fast as a rocket, leaping straight up into the air to overcome any obstacle in search of new adventure!

His quest for adventure would sometimes overcome his desire to please, and he would not return to voice command. He just couldn't help himself. The gas station would call, "I have Friday here." A stranger on the next street would call, "I have Friday here." The police in the next town would call, "We have Friday here." The woman with the chicken coop would call, "I have Friday here."

One day I returned from searching by car for Friday in the surrounding area to no avail. I was pacing the living room, and looked out the window as the garbage truck pulled up. There was Friday sitting in the passenger seat! The driver opened the door, and Friday looked back as though to say, "Thanks for the lift!"

He loved the outdoors. When he was lying in the snow for hours, I would worry and want to bring him in. He would say, "No, I am enjoying the fresh snow, dreaming my dreams of the past and the future." I would insist and tug on his rope, he would resist and go limp. He knew best.

How did this gentle giant emerge and survive the oppression of his former life? How did he know to respond to a treat, taking it from our fingers with the slightest touch rather than a bite? How did he respond to our love so readily when he was mistreated in his early life? How did he learn to trust so readily that even when he went to the vet he would jump onto the examining table, believing we all were helping him? What was it that allowed him to be the optimist when his other life taught him nothing but neglect and negativity? I have wondered that for years.

Scott eventually met and married Christina. Scott, Christina, and Friday moved away; and he won the hearts of everyone he met. Christina comes from a big, loving Italian family, and Friday enjoyed freshly grated Parmesan cheese and home-made spaghetti sauce over his food. He became an Italian dog. He loved his extended family and the adventure of new surroundings and new friends. Everyone loved him, young and old. He was about eight or nine years old then, and it was his first encounter with small children. He allowed them to climb and crawl on him with never a complaint. When he tired of them he would come and sit close to Scott, leaning on him as if to say, "Rescue me." Christina's grandmother was eighty-five years old when she died. Her last words to Christina were, "Take care of Friday."

The end of this part of life's adventure came not long ago. He had the best care that love and money could give most of his life, but his athletic body gave out to incurable illness. Even through all his days of hospitalization, he trusted that everyone around him had only the best intentions toward him. When he was given his final injection to give him peace from his illness, he looked to Scott and reached out his paw as though to say, "It's been great, hasn't it? Thanks for the lift!"

Friday leaves behind many things. He leaves a house filled with his warmth and his toys to welcome a new dog rescued from the animal shelter named Tommi, after Christina's grandmother. He leaves a bit of his exuberance and sense of adventure with each of us. He touched us with his indomitable spirit to live and love no matter what happened. His ashes are scattered in the woods in Massachusetts where he loved to run. There he leaves his memory to all living things: "I was here, I lived life every minute, I loved every minute . . . enjoy!" He leaves a legacy of love and laughter. He leaves proof that even when growing up with neglect and oppression it is possible to live and love. After all, the more love and loyalty you give, the more you get.

from OUR BEST FRIENDS

Friday: A Son's Story

SCOTT FORBIS

BIG HEADED GULLUTE
BIG HEADED MONSTER
CIRCUS DOG
FRI DOG
FRY
FRYGUY
FRYMASTER
FRYMONSTER
FRYSTER
FUR FACE
GRANDOG
HAPPY DOG
HOUND DOGGIE
HOUNDSTER
KING FRYDAY
KING BUDDIE
KING DOGGIE
KING BOY
LEAPER DOG
MR. FEROCIOUS
MR. PATIENCE
MR. FUR BETWEEN YOUR TOES CAN'T WAIT FOR
    ME TO GET READY TO Go OUTSIDE

MY LITTLE BUDDY
MR. POLITE BOY
PRANCER DOG
RUFFA DUFFA
SHOVEL PAW
SILLY MANAMULE
SNOW DOG
SQUIRREL HUNTER
THE HUNTER DOG
THE KING
THE SWAMP THING

MADE Us LAUGH
MADE Us CRY
MADE Us WORRY
MADE Us HAPPY
MADE Us SAD
MADE Us WONDER
MADE Us SMILE

WE ARE FORTUNATE
HE WAS FORTUNATE
HE Is THE KING

I MISS HIM
WE MISS HIM

I AM SAD

from OUR BEST FRIENDS

Mr. Personality

FRANCYNE ANDERSON

$\mathcal{M}$y friend is suffering. A very essential part of her happiness is in pain. She cannot let go, and neither can Buttons. So, at night, my friend sleeps on the floor beside her beloved, thirteen-year-old Dalmatian. My friend calls her, "My heart."

There are times when Buttons cannot get up. She wants to, but, like us humans, the mind is willing and the body is weak. My friend spends the night beside her, and during the day she keeps constant watch, for fear that death will come and she won't be there to tell her goodbye.

Everyone who knows me says I'm not an animal lover. Should I tell them why? It isn't that I dislike animals. Rather, it's that I have refused to love them. I didn't fully understand that until I was forced to look at my friend's situation, and then the memory of an old hurt surfaced.

When I was a kid, probably about six years old, we got a white, part-Scottish terrier puppy, a ball of fur with a beautiful pointed face and a long straight coat. We lived on a farm at the time and, even at six weeks old, he ruled the roost. We named him Pat, but we should have called him Mr. Personality.

My dad owned several greyhounds and Pat quickly made them toe the line. When we moved into town three years later, he continued to be boss of the yard. We lived on a corner lot and he'd stand guard in my mother's flower bed, to be sure the greyhounds went around to the side street to get to their pen.

Pat was a scrappy little thing. The barber shop was a block and a half from our house, and a gathering place for the retired men of the community. They all had great "Pat" stories. He patrolled the sidewalks, they said, and if other dogs didn't run when he barked at them, he'd disappear. Then, in a few minutes, he'd come back with the greyhounds and they would fight his battle. Of course, he'd beat it back to the house, so he could be there to insure that they wouldn't try to go through the yard.

Pat loved to play hide-and-seek, and he understood about taking turns hiding or staying at the base. We would say, "Okay, Pat go hide." And he'd run lickety-split to a hiding hole. As soon as one of us saw him, the race was on to get back to home base first. Of course, he won. Then he'd stand there and let us go hide.

We always figured Pat was there to protect us. Heaven knows, we weren't confronted with the dangers that the children of today face, but he made us feel safe and loved. Foolishly, we took his life for granted, thinking he wouldn't ever leave us.

One night he started a fight he couldn't win, and when I went to check the mail before school the next morning one of the men in the post office told me he thought our dog was dead in the alley. I argued with the logic of a twelve-year-old: "Pat wouldn't die," I told the man. When he realized how upset I was, he said, "Well, maybe it isn't your dog, but why don't you go take a look?"

Yes, it was Pat. I ran down the alley toward our house, wailing all the way. That afternoon, after school, my dad dug a hole and we buried Pat in the bassinet both my brother and I had slept in as infants.

It took looking at the pain in my friend's face, seeing the fear of the grief to come in her eyes, to make me realize that the experience of losing Pat had made me more than just cautious when it came to falling in love with a puppy. With sudden clarity, I understood that I feared another dog would be reckless, as Pat had been. If I never got another dog, then I'd never experience the pain of losing him again.

My defenses were in place and my heart was well guarded. Yet I thought of the love my friend has shared with her Dalmatian, the memories she will have to comfort her during her grief. Then a thought came to my mind: Would I want a docile puppy? Would I want one with less personality than Mr. Personality, himself? The answer was a resounding "No."

Today, I'm thinking that a small Dachshund, feisty and playful, would be perfect for me.

The Outcast

LEE EBLER

$\mathcal{S}$ometimes, in the farm world, animals are rejected by their own kind. That's what happened to Herman the duck.

Herman came to us one cold spring morning on a bitter wind. This same wind had awakened Brother and me, and we had lain upstairs under the slanted ceiling and listened. Eventually the gale gentled, and from somewhere high overhead came the sound of ducks.

"Going north toward the pond," said Brother sleepily. It wasn't until after breakfast that we found the wind had left a gift.

The duck was in the barnyard, crouching by the plow. He looked dazed, and not even Grandpa had seen a more oddly-put-together bird.

"Funny lookin'," said Grandpa. "Maybe part wild, part domestic."

The duck stood up. He was ungainly, tall and narrow, with mottled black, white, and brown feathers. He had soulful dark eyes and a long, thin neck. He was the ugly duck that would never be a swan.

"Squawk!" said the duck, in an anxious, unducklike voice.

"Sounds like part chicken, too," said Grandma dryly.

"He's hurt," said Brother. "See how he's holding his wing."

"Might let him mend a few days in the old brooder house,"

said Grandpa. "Probably got left when that flock flew over."

He started toward the duck, but to his surprise, the duck came to him, still squawking. Grandpa picked him up.

"Fusses like a baby," said Grandma. "Probably be no end of trouble." Then to Brother and me: "You want to keep him?"

We nodded.

"Then he's your responsibility. But I suspect he's a duck that'll need lookin' after."

Grandma named the duck Herman because he reminded her of a former suitor, although she was careful not to divulge any romantic particulars.

Herman was an original. Grandma had guessed right about him. He was high-strung, prone to trouble, overly anxious to make friends, and he loved people. During his convalescence in the brooder house, he fussed until Brother or I paid him a visit.

"He was surely once a house duck," said Brother. "He wears a person out wanting to be close. But it'll be easier when we can let him loose."

Brother and I understood that Herman would have a period of adjustment to the farm's caste system, where every animal had a social position. But eventually, we figured, he'd fit in. Then we'd get a break.

As soon as Herman's wing healed, we introduced him to the two farm ducks. Herman was ecstatic. He penguin-walked toward them, squawking happily. The ducks took one look at Herman and hissed. Herman was saved from annihilation by Brother brandishing the rake.

"Just needs time," Grandpa said.

But without exception, every animal rejected Herman. Even the little baretailed banty hen—who was at the absolute bottom of the pecking order—flew at him. Herman's oddness and lack of fowlish common sense seemed to set him apart. Herman was an outcast.

"What can you expect," asked Grandma, "from a duck who chokes on crab apples, gets locked in a farrowing shed with a mad sow, and generally makes himself a nuisance?"

"What happens if we get tired of bailing Herman out of trouble?" I asked Grandma the afternoon we spent chasing him from the garden.

"Roast duck," she replied, not looking up from the bluing tub.

There followed a time when we encouraged Herman to fly away by launching him from the smokehouse roof. Although Herman flew well, he did not fly far. Usually he circled back and waited for us to climb down. By the middle of summer, we were seeing Herman the first thing in the morning and the last thing at night.

"That flock of ducks probably jilted him on purpose," said Grandma.

Then, in late August, Herman began to change. His soulful eyes had a faraway look, and he often went off to swim in solitary circles on the pond. At other times, we would find him looking northward, waiting. When the fall migration started, we understood.

When he heard the flocks, Herman would become agitated, not wanting his food, not wanting the lonesome security of the brooder house, not wanting us. We surprised ourselves then by worrying about him, and once we even asked Grandpa to clip his wings.

"But you tried to make him leave," reminded Grandpa. Then after thinking it over: "I'll clip him, if that's really what you want."

We didn't know what we wanted. If Herman left, we'd have peace, and yet his tragicomic figure had become an important part of our lives.

"You know," said Brother, after a long discussion. "we've spent a hard summer mostly rescuing Herman, and that's kinda clipped our wings. Herman doesn't know any better, but I guess we do." So the matter of wing clipping was dropped.

When the first flock arrived on the pond, Herman made his familiar, too-eager advances. Brother and I, watching from the hickory tree, saw two ducks warn him off. But Herman was not discouraged. In the following days, he often hurried to the pond when a flock landed, but he was always back in the brooder house the next morning, sadder if not wiser. We resigned ourselves to Herman forever.

Then one day a strange little band of ducks flew over, and Herman saw them. He recently had stopped even going to the pond, but something about this flock seemed to stir him. He headed north, with Brother and me following at a distance.

There were five ducks on the pond, and they were a scruffy mixture of mallards and mud ducks and heaven only knew what else.

"Squawk!" called Herman. Bad experiences forgotten, he waddled toward them and slipped into the water.

There was a moment of silence. The other ducks looked at Herman. Herman looked at them. Brother and I held our breath. Then the lead duck casually bent his head into the water. The other ducks followed. Herman swam around them, his circles getting smaller and smaller. Then suddenly he was no longer on the outside of the group. He was part of it.

"He did it!" whispered Brother. "I just hope he doesn't

bring 'em back to the brooder house. Wouldn't Grandma have a hissy fit?"

Herman did not return to the brooder house that night or the next. And Grandpa kept us away so Herman could cement his acceptance.

On the third day, we saw the small ragtag group fly over the farm. There were six of them now. They seemed both brave and funny, and a bitter wind was at their backs.

Grandpa shook his head. "Goin' north," he said. "Leave it to Herman to fall in with a bunch with no sense of direction."

"Will he be OK?" I asked. I had expected to be mostly relieved when Herman left, but somehow I felt as empty as the brooder house.

"I don't know," said Grandpa, giving no dishonest comfort.

Brother and I felt lost all that day, and in the chill of sunset, Grandpa walked us down to the pond. It was serene and empty.

"Herman found his own kind," said Grandpa at last. "He fits in. He's not an outcast. You can't wish anything better for him."

"Seems like the summer was a loss," said Brother. He broke off a milkweed stalk and opened the dried pod.

"You learned from Herman," Grandpa said slowly. "You learned to stick with a job, though you didn't like it. You learned feelin's aren't simple. You liked Herman, and you didn't like him. But you cared about him, because you gave to him. Learnin's never a loss. Now he's free, and you're free. No clipped wings. Seems like Herman gave you a lot."

Well, maybe he had.

Brother held up the milkweed and shook it. The cold wind sent the silky parachutes flying upward.

No clipped wings.

from COUNTRY LIVING

The Truth About Snoopy

CHRISTIE CRAIG

The fact that he was white with brown and black spots made the name Snoopy appropriate enough. He did, however, have a little beagle in him. Then again he also had a little of various other breeds. And that, my father told me, made him a "sooner." "Sooner be one kind than another," Daddy would say.

Daddy swore he'd never known another dog to be such a total klutz. Daddy also said if it wasn't for bad luck, that dog wouldn't have no luck at all. To call Snoopy accident-prone would be an understatement. So, as my love for the puppy grew, so did the vet bills.

Daddy wasn't too thrilled with that. As an independent contractor in the early sixties, in a small southern town, times were hard for him. He'd only consented to getting the dog after Mama convinced him there were enough table scraps and we wouldn't have to purchase dog food.

As it turned out it was the vet bills we couldn't afford. At only a few months old, Snoopy came home with a swollen eye and Daddy relented. We took the dog to the vet. I thought Snoopy looked rather cute wearing the temporary eye patch; Daddy didn't seem to appreciate it.

A few months later, Snoopy hobbled home with a broken leg, and Daddy relented again. The vet got the money intended for the electric bill that month.

Winter rolled around, and the cold, wet weather meant less work for Daddy, which meant money was harder to come by. So when Snoopy started acting puny, Daddy said this was one time that dog would just have to tough it out. After a change of diet—purchased dog food—Snoopy was fine.

The next weekend Snoopy got one of those five-hooked fishing lures caught in his mouth. Being Sunday, the only vet open was the after-hours clinic, which Daddy explained "cost an arm and a leg."

You'd think Snoopy would have learned a lesson along the way, but we were never so lucky. And as Daddy put it, neither was Snoopy. Several months later my pet got into a fight. He came home with a ripped ear. Mama doctored him but the ear never did grow back together. So along with Snoopy's other scars, he had a split ear.

Scarred or not, I still loved that dog. We would spend most of the humid afternoons sitting on the back porch steps, waiting for an occasional breeze, which would always smell like Mama's roses. Snoopy would lay his soft head on my lap and gaze up at me with those soulful, loving eyes.

Then one day I found Snoopy hiding under Daddy's truck. Those soulful eyes looked pathetic. I'd become familiar with that down-on-my-luck expression. When I crawled under the truck, the smell of leaky oil and old tires made my nose wrinkle, and the gravel cut into my bare knees.

It was bad that time. I ran to get Mama. Daddy was gone that day and I felt relieved. Too many times I'd heard my father's threat: "We can't afford this dog. We gotta' get rid of him."

Mama looked at the injury and frowned. "We've got to take him to a doctor," I pleaded.

"Honey, there's no money," she said and petted the animal. She stared at the dog for a few minutes, then at me. "Do you think he would bite you?"

"Snoopy would never bite me," I told her, wiping the tears from my eyes.

Convinced, she left me with Snoopy while she went to get supplies. She came back with a needle, fishing line, medicine and bandages.

She doused Snoopy's wound with alcohol and the pungent smell hung in the air. Then the cold fire-inducing liquid ran down my scraped knees and tears filled my eyes. I cried for myself that hot August day. But mostly, I cried for Snoopy. He whimpered, tried to get away, but he never, ever, tried to bite me.

The only problem Mama couldn't work out was how to get a bandage on him. The stitches would tear open if she couldn't find a way to protect them.

Suddenly, she smiled and went back inside. She came out with an old girdle. She cut the legs off and we slipped it over the dog's head and secured it around his belly. When Daddy came home that day I saw the look on his face. "It didn't cost you anything," I told him.

As it turned out, Snoopy was okay. But the poor animal became the laughing stock of the neighborhood. It seemed no one had ever seen a dog wearing a girdle before.

Not long after that I spent the night away. When I got home, Snoopy didn't come running. I called, walked the streets, but I came back alone. Fearing the worst, I went to find Daddy. The sound of the table saw led me to the garage. In a

THE TRUTH ABOUT SNOOPY

cloud of scented sawdust, tears already forming in my eyes, I stood waiting for the roar of the machine to stop.

"Where is he?" I asked. "Tell me you didn't give him away." Daddy slowly set the piece of lumber to the side and then confessed that he'd found a good home for Snoopy.

I think that was the first time I ever felt disappointed in my dad. I cried for weeks. Even at eight years old I knew it wasn't right for someone to give away something that didn't belong to him. Snoopy had been my dog!

Months later, I had to write a personal experience paper for second-grade English. I wrote about Snoopy and how I would *never* forgive my daddy for giving him away. I got a B+ on that paper and I made sure I brought it home.

Watching my dad read it that night at the supper table, I saw his eyes, the hurt so apparent. I felt a little guilty, but it felt good, too. Revenge can be satisfying, even for a child.

Daddy dropped the paper on the table. "Someday, you'll understand," he whispered and then he left without eating.

Years passed. I eventually did forgive my dad, but I never forgot.

Recently, as I visited my father, my six-year-old son sat in his grandpa's lap and listened as he recounted a few of my childhood episodes. The last story he told was about a spotted dog who'd worn a girdle. My son, so intrigued with the story, asked the obvious questions. "Where's Snoopy now? What happened to him?"

Daddy's eyes met mine. We simply stared. Finally I answered my son's question. "We had to give him away to a better home," I said, hoping I'd managed to keep the sting from my voice. Even after almost thirty years, I still felt wronged.

My daddy cleared his throat. "I never gave your dog away.

He got hit by a car. I told the vet to do everything he could to save him, but that dog was a goner. Even in dying, that animal cost me a fortune." Daddy smiled, but that smile didn't appear too genuine.

I remembered the look of hurt that had filled my father's eyes when he'd read my school paper. Tears filled my throat. "Why didn't you tell me?"

He took a deep breath. "I was afraid it would break your heart. I just thought if you believed the dog was alive, it wouldn't hurt so much."

"You should have told me," I repeated. Daddy just shook his head and changed the subject, a sign his emotions were too close to the surface.

Looking back, I honestly believe the truth wouldn't have hurt either of us as much as that lie did. Nevertheless, Daddy said that someday I would understand. Now I do.

Right or wrong, Daddy lied to protect me. As a parent, I've skirted around a few truths, told a few lies myself. Someday, my son will learn that there really isn't a goldfish heaven. I think I'll be more careful how I handle those difficult situations. But yes, my daddy *was* right. I do understand.

My Bestest Friend

MARY M. ALWARD

$\mathcal{I}$ grew up on a farm in southern Ontario. Animals and fowl were a part of everyday life. The old Banty rooster crowed each morning as the sun peeked over the horizon. He would stand on the split rail fence, flap his colorful wings, stretch his neck and let out a Cock-a-doodle-doo that woke everyone in the house, as well as the barnyard animals.

Our house stood on a lot of land in the corner of my maternal grandparent's hundred-acre farm. I spent much of my childhood surrounded by the farm animals and had no reason to fear any of them. Cows, horses, chickens, ducks, turkeys, pigs and even Oscar, the cantankerous Holstein bull, filled my days with joy.

Between Grandma's house and the old red barn, stood a gas tank that supplied fuel for Grandpa's Massey Harris tractors. Beside that tank, Prince, the German Shepherd watchdog stood guard over the precious gasoline. Prince had a regal look, which gave evidence to the name that he'd been given. Though he would snarl and make a terrible fuss when strangers visited, Prince was a wonderful playmate for a young girl with bright red hair.

Each day, I would visit Prince. I loved nothing better than to sit on the ground between his feet and scratch his ears or

187

stroke his shiny coat. Prince loved my visits. He would lay his head on my lap, close his eyes and bask in the attention I heaped upon him.

I adored Prince and loved to take him his daily meal, which Grandma fed him in early afternoon. I would hold his shiny tin dish in small, baby hands and carefully walk down the lane to the doghouse. Prince eagerly waited for me to put the dish down. He never growled or gave any sign of aggression. I would stand back and wait for him to finish wolfing down his food. Then, I would scratch his ears and talk to him in a soft, soothing voice.

One day, Grandpa brought home a puppy. I didn't like him. He was fat and ugly and didn't have the regal manner of Prince. I overheard Grandpa telling Grandma that Prince was getting old and he wanted the new pup to spend time with Prince. This would teach him to be a good watchdog, as Prince was one of the best.

The fact that Prince was getting old and going to die didn't particularly bother me. On a farm, death is a part of life. I learned at a young age to accept the inevitable.

The new puppy was allowed to wander in the yard but being young, he tended to stay close to Prince. At first, Prince didn't seem to mind the intruder but then the pup began to bite his ears and tail when the elderly dog fell asleep. Prince would yelp in pain, then lunge into the air, snapping at the younger dog. This would send the pup scurrying, tail between his legs.

One warm afternoon in May, Grandma asked me if I would like to feed Prince. Would I? Did she need to ask? I was delighted and danced with excitement as she prepared Prince's food.

As Grandma handed me Prince's bowl, she cautioned me

not to step on his paw or touch him if he was sleeping. I was to set the bowl on the ground and return to the house. I agreed to do as she said and set off down the lane.

When I arrived at my destination, Prince was lying on the packed earth, fast asleep. I remember wondering why Grandma had warned me not to step on Prince's paw. I had no fear of the dog. He would never hurt me.

Being an adventurous child who had no fear of the farm animals, I poised my foot in the air and brought it firmly down on Prince's paw. Prince lunged into the air, snarling. He swung his head. As he did this, his fang caught the side of my face.

Grandma heard my cries and came running. She found me sitting on the ground, Prince standing over me, licking my face. He was whining and crying. She and Dad took me to the hospital twenty miles away, leaving my mother, who was eight months pregnant, at home.

Two hours later, we were back. I had seventeen stitches in my face. After reassuring Mom that I was fine, I headed for Grandma's.

"Where are you going?" Mom called.

"I'm going to see Prince," I answered, still heading in the direction of Grandma's.

"Stop! I don't think that is a good idea," Mom said.

"But Mom . . . Prince didn't mean to hurt me. I need to let him know I'm okay. He's my bestest friend in the whole world."

I heard my father say quietly, "Let her go. It won't hurt her to see Prince and if we don't let her go, she may fear dogs all of her life."

I climbed up the hill to Grandma's and ran down the lane as fast as my short, chubby legs would carry me. Prince was standing in front of his doghouse. When he saw me, he began to dance on his back legs, tail wagging excitedly. I wrapped my arms around his neck, hugging him tight. He washed every inch of my baby face with his tongue. I accepted his licking as kisses of apology.

I will never forget that day. When I was older, Grandma told me that when she arrived on the scene, Prince was crying real tears. She said it was the only time in her life she had seen tears stream from the eyes of an animal.

Today, I don't even realize that there is a scar on the right side of my face unless someone mentions it. It has been a part of me almost as long as I can remember. If someone asks what happened, I reply, "It was a present given to me by my best friend."

In a way, I am glad that Prince gave me that scar on my face. It is the symbol of true friendship—the symbol of forgiveness that only a child could give to her "bestest friend." It is a symbol of unconditional love between animal and human.

One day, when I pass from this earthly plane I hope to meet Prince once again. Hopefully, I will once again climb that hill to Grandma's and run down the lane to visit Prince, my "bestest friend."

Klutz

KRISTIN VON KREISLER

$\mathcal{W}$hen Lisa Funderburk gave birth to Lyndsey, her daughter, she worried that her dachshund-beagle mutt Klutz would be jealous. She needn't have worried. Klutz became even more fiercely devoted to Lyndsey than he was to Lisa, even though he'd lived with Lisa for the past eight years.

If Lyndsey wailed in her crib, Klutz ran to Lisa, bit her pant leg, and tugged her to the baby. If Lisa did not respond immediately, the dog ran in circles around her and barked. Klutz was just as protective when Lyndsey tried to crawl up the stairs; he grabbed her by the seat of her pants and pulled her back to safety. Lyndsey, he clearly felt, was his personal charge.

Just before Christmas, when the child was three years old, she got up from the kitchen table in Lehigh Acres, Florida. "I'm going to let Klutzie in," she said.

She opened the door to the backyard and called Klutz, but he did not heave himself up from his daily sunning spot in the grass as he normally would. Nor did he waddle on his short little legs across the threshold. Lyndsey started out the door to get him but suddenly stopped when he jumped up, barking and yapping at her.

Klutz continued to bark, and his paws thudded against the ground again and again, as if he were jumping on something.

Neither Lisa nor her parents got up from the table to check on him until his barks turned suddenly to shrieks, then to piercing, angry yelps. Lisa ran to the door, pushed Lyndsey aside, and heard a rattling sound, as if someone were shaking dice in a tin can. A rattlesnake was coiled under a bush and ready to strike.

"Get back!" Lisa screamed to Klutz.

It was too late. The dog stopped yelping and collapsed on the ground. But he still seemed determined to protect Lyndsey from the snake. He lurched to his feet and staggered toward it, then fell to his stomach. He raised himself up again and crawled toward the snake. Once more the rattler struck.

Lisa froze. Her heart seemed to stop beating. She couldn't watch her beloved dog die before her eyes without trying to save him.

She grabbed her car keys. To keep from passing the snake to reach Klutz, she ran out the front door and around the house to the back, where Klutz lay foaming at the mouth. Though he was unable to stand, he wouldn't give up. He still flailed his paws at the snake and tried to fight it.

Lisa picked up the dog, rushed to her car, and lay him on the seat beside her. As she sped two miles to the nearest veterinary clinic, she begged Klutz, "Don't die! Please, don't die!" Christmas was coming, she reminded him. "You have to open your presents. I've bought you a new bed and a squeaky toy. Don't die!"

Klutz, scarcely able to breathe, trembled violently. His eyes rolled back in his head, and he went into convulsions.

How could she help him? Whenever *she* was sick, Klutz always climbed on her and refused to leave until she felt better. He was so emotionally connected to her that once he'd even known that she was delirious when she was miles from home in an emergency room. At just the moment she'd called his name in the hospital, he had "heard" her at home and scratched her bedroom door so fiercely that his paws bled. What could she possibly do now to repay him for his devotion?

In the clinic, Dr. Darry Griebel set Klutz on a steel table and examined him. The snake had bitten him twice, on his eyelid and in his eyeball. Griebel measured four inches between each fang mark.

As a snake grows older and larger, its fangs get farther apart, he told Lisa. "That snake had to be huge. At least five feet."

The bigger the snake, the more venom it has in its bite, he explained. And the older the dog, the less strength it has to fight for its life. At age eleven, Klutz was at a great disadvantage.

"I'm not sure we ought to try and save him," Griebel said sadly.

"We *have* to try," Lisa argued. "Do anything you can. I don't care how much it costs."

Griebel gave Klutz intravenous antibiotics and two shots of antivenin, then put him in a cage to keep a careful watch on him.

"The first forty-eight hours will be the most dangerous," he warned. "If he doesn't die in two days, he'll probably make it."

Lisa loved Klutz so much that she was not sure *she* would make it. Two days would seem like two years. She sat beside his cage with tears rolling down her face and remembered all the times when he had licked them off her cheeks.

"You can't die this way," she told Klutz again and again. "I couldn't stand it if you died trying to save Lyndsey."

Klutz tried to turn his head to lick her hand but couldn't. His head and neck had swollen to the size of a St. Bernard's; his whole body had ballooned out of shape. He closed his eyes and retreated into himself, miles away in a world of pain.

Lisa got up to leave, so he could rest. "You have to make it," she whispered. "You have to come home."

She returned to her house for her mother's credit card to pay Griebel (and she learned that her father had killed the snake with a shovel). On her way back to the clinic, she bought Klutz a teddy bear and hung a medal with a heart and two praying hands around his neck. When she put the bear in the cage beside Klutz, he opened his eyes and tried to scoot closer to her—but he could not move. He whimpered. Tears wet Lisa's cheeks.

The next day she returned with special meals that her mother had cooked and packed in plastic containers: spaghetti and meatballs, browned hamburger and rice, scrambled eggs, and apple pie. For the first time since Klutz had come to the clinic, he ate—not voraciously, but with interest. The first twenty-four of his forty-eight hours of danger had passed.

The next twenty-four hours were also uneventful. Klutz seemed to be winning his fight for survival. His swelling went down enough that he could sit on his plump little haunches or stand with his stomach hanging, as always, just inches from the ground. He held out his paws to Lisa.

She patted him. "You're such a wonderful dog."

Though he appeared much better, she did not bring Lyndsey to visit him for a few days. Lisa worried that his puffy face and weakness might upset her daughter. But by Christmas Eve, he seemed to have improved so much that the doctor said Klutz could go home. Alert and eager, he trotted across the clinic's grass to Lisa's car.

When the dog got home and first saw Lyndsey, he whined joyfully, wagged his tail, and licked her. Lisa put him on pillows and blankets in a playpen, so Lyndsey could sit outside it and talk to him. Whenever she left the room, Klutz, unable to follow, cried so plaintively that she hurried back. She sang to him and chattered about Christmas.

Just before midnight, the family left for mass to thank God that Klutz seemed to be recovering. When they got home, however, he was sick again. He was panting, scarcely able to breathe. His heart was beating harder than normal, and his eyes were glazed. For the rest of the night, Lisa stayed with him, patted him, and prayed for him.

On Christmas morning she called Griebel. "Klutz doesn't look so good." The lump in her throat felt like a boulder.

"Bring him to my office. I'll meet you there."

Lisa was amazed that even on Christmas, Griebel was willing to leave his family in order to help Klutz. He picked up the dog and laid him on the examination table.

"He's having complications from the antivenin," Griebel determined. "He needs a blood transfusion."

After that, nothing more could be done for him, except to wait and see what happened.

The waiting was agony for Lisa, Lyndsey, Lisa's parents, and Griebel. At four o'clock the next morning, Klutz died.

At six o'clock, Griebel, who had not left Klutz for nearly twenty-four hours, called Lisa and told her Klutz was gone. "He gave his life for Lyndsey," he said.

Lyndsey weighed twenty-eight pounds, exactly Klutz's weight. Getting her to the hospital—five miles farther away than Griebel's clinic—in time to save her life would have been impossible. If she'd been bitten, she would have died. Klutz had attacked the snake, so she would live.

Klutz had also fought to stay alive as long as he could for

Lyndsey's sake. "He must have been determined to go back home and make sure she was all right," Griebel told Lisa. "Once he knew that, then he could die."

Klutz had died knowing that he'd succeeded in protecting Lyndsey.

from THE COMPASSION OF ANIMALS

Everything Happens for a Reason

JANET CLAYTON

---

*I*t was May and both my sons—Kevin, age six, and Cameron, age four—were looking forward to the arrival of their new kittens. As Sassy, our Siamese cat got bigger, the boys had questions about the birth. After explaining it to them, I decided that if the opportunity came, I'd let the boys watch and experience the miracle themselves.

When the time came, I allowed them to be present, but too late I realized that the lesson they gained was not the one I'd hoped for. All but one of Sassy's kittens were stillborn, and some very tough questions about life and death began forming in my sons' minds. That evening their dad, Stephen, sat the boys down and talked to them.

"Why?" they asked.

Stephen shook his head and I'll never forget his words: "Everything happens for a reason. Sometimes we just don't understand."

That afternoon we buried the kittens in a special spot in our backyard. I remember thinking that, like the boys, I didn't understand.

A week later, the surviving kitten also died. This death was the hardest for the boys to understand and accept. Once again their dad came to the rescue. His casual manner and gentle voice brought comfort and peace to their hearts. As they buried the last kitten, I listened from the distance as he told them about God, about how he wasn't sure if animals went to heaven, but he sure hoped so. He told them about his vision of heaven, about how it was even a better place than earth. "We might miss them, but we shouldn't be sad too long," he said.

The boys somehow came to a gentle acceptance, and in the next few days, things went back to normal. The boys often made little remarks about the kittens, saying that they weren't really gone, they were with God. The images they built were so peaceful, they brought comfort to my own heart.

Stephen had told the boys everything happens for a reason, but who would have guessed that two days later I would have to lead the boys back to that special spot in our yard and tell them that their father, only forty-three years old, had died suddenly of a heart attack?

My oldest started crying and I held him tight. Cameron stood frozen, tears brimming his brown eyes. Then his little voice broke the silence. "Daddy's with the kittens."

While I held my boys that sad moment, they talked about kittens, heaven and about their dad being with God. I realized how right Stephen had been. Everything happens for a reason. Whether he'd known it or not, Stephen had helped his sons accept his untimely death.

While I do not believe God intentionally took the lives of those kittens, I believe God uses each situation, good or bad, happy or sad, to prepare us for what is ahead. His gentle hand is always upon us.

An Answered Prayer

CHRISTIE CRAIG

I was eleven but Mama still tucked me in at night. I would close my eyes and say my prayers. "God bless Mama, Daddy…" and on a day that my two male siblings hadn't teased me too much, I'd tag on, "and my brothers, too." Then in a real desperate voice I would always add, "And please God, let me have a pet."

I knew I was praying to God, but in my young mind I figured it wouldn't hurt for Mama to know my heart's desire. I figured sooner or later God would intervene and Mama would give in and take me to the pet store with the intention to buy. I envisioned the cute little puppy that would chase balls or that I could train to shake hands. Or maybe one of those cuddly, furry kittens that Mama said would shed everywhere.

It was a few months later when we came home from school and she announced she had a surprise for us. From the look on her face I knew she thought it was real special and my mind went straight to that puppy or kitten. But when Mama led us into the kitchen where a large aquarium set on the table I was a bit disappointed. I hadn't had a lot of pet experience, but I knew puppies or kittens didn't come in aquariums.

Upon closer inspection my mood soured even more. "What is it?" I asked and jumped back.

Mama explained that my uncle had brought over the three-foot iguana because a friend of his couldn't keep it anymore. "It didn't cost us anything," she said.

"But it's ugly!" I insisted. "Give it back!"

Of course my brothers didn't share my feelings. They thought the large lizard was the best pet in the world. They named him Godzilla and within a few hours they had the lizard sitting on their shoulders and hand feeding it fruit cocktail. All I could think was that God had made a big mistake. He hadn't understood. Didn't He know when I asked for a pet, I wanted a dog or a kitten? Even a hamster would have suited me. But a lizard?

Needless to say, my brothers didn't get an argument from me when they insisted the lizard take up residence in their room. I didn't care for the ugly, scaly creature—didn't want to hold it—didn't want it near me. It was their pet. Not mine. I still had some praying to do!

For the next few weeks I watched my brothers make the most of having a pet that the majority of people wouldn't touch. Time after time I'd witness as they would walk into a room with Godzilla on their shoulders. At first people would just assume it was one of those big plastic toys. But then the creature would turn its head and suddenly you'd hear the screams that would eventually turn to laughter. I admit, I even found it funny at first. Then something happened.

Perhaps it was because I noticed that the only time they held the creature was when someone new came over. Perhaps it was because I'd been on the laughing end of too many of their jokes, or because too many kids teased me about being a slightly overweight child. Whatever the reason, I began to feel sorry for Godzilla. Maybe he didn't want to be laughed at either.

When my brothers weren't around I'd sneak into their room and study the scaly creature in his aquarium. I would look at him and he would look at me. I never got too close. After a few weeks I noticed more times than not the lizard would be without food or water. Finally I did what every responsible, and bright eleven-year-old girl would do. I tattled.

Mother's answer was simple. "Then feed it."

Trying to feed an animal you didn't want to touch wasn't all that easy. Once when I reached in to get the bowl Godzilla turned and bumped my hand with his nose. I jumped. So did Godzilla. After a good laugh, I felt braver. I slowly reached in and touched the lizard on the top of his head. He didn't feel as yucky as I'd thought he would. So I stroked him again. The lizard, as if starved for attention, closed his eyes and rubbed his head against my palm.

After several more times of finding the animal without food, I decided to teach my brothers a lesson. I moved Godzilla to my room. I was certain they would come home and repent. But they never even realized he was gone. When I told them they were simply glad to be free of the responsibility.

So Godzilla and I became roommates. He would sit with me on my bed when I did my homework. He would climb on my shoulder and expect to be hand fed. When he would feel neglected he'd come over and bump my hand for me to give him a stroke. Godzilla wasn't a puppy. He couldn't chase balls or shake hands. But he taught me that love isn't about what's on the outside, but what's on the inside—it isn't about what they can do for you, but about what you can do for them. No, Godzilla wasn't the pet I'd dreamed about. He was more. He was an answered prayer. Looking back, I think God understood exactly what I needed all along.

A Time for Love

MARY CHAVOUSTIE

7t seemed like only yesterday that we had lost a family member. "A seizure," the vet had said. "German Shepherds are known for that. There's nothing you could have done."

Three tearful months passed and the question of a new dog came more frequently from Eric, our eight-year-old son. Daily I'd be met by a pouty frown and a question. "But when, Mom?" he'd say. "When?"

"It's not the right time," I'd reply. "Not yet." And deep down I wondered, *Would there ever be another time? Could I ever let myself care that much about another animal . . . again?*

Weekdays seemed to pass more quickly with everyone off to work or school; it was the weekends that seemed the longest. Saturday house cleaning would inevitably uncover a rawhide chew from beneath the sofa, a ball from behind a chair, or even a morsel of dog food stranded in a corner, each a soulful reminder of our beloved pet. One such weekend arrived and I decided a movie might lift everyone's spirits. "You pick," I told Eric. Delighted, he came running back with the newspaper, pointing proudly to the premiere of a remake of the well-loved movie, *Lassie.* Maybe, I thought, a dog movie would be good therapy for all of us, even for Don, the seemingly stoic husband and father who also felt the loss.

As the three of us drove along the busy two-lane road to the mall, our eyes caught a glimpse of a weak and bedraggled dog climbing up from the ditch. She stumbled onto the asphalt, then stared, motionless, into our bumper. The screech of our brakes seemed to amplify the gasp of my voice.

Ribs protruded from the dog's belly as she nimbly shifted from one burr-laden paw to another. Her lifeless coat was tangled with briars and weeks of debris. She glared at us with dark, sunken eyes, ears lowered.

"I know! I know!" said Don. "I'm pulling over. I know you want to go see about her. Just be careful."

From years past, he knew his warning was falling on deaf ears; I was never "careful" about animals. I believed, naively, they could seldom be dangerous, only hungry or hurt or homeless. I sensed the ragged collie was all three.

I opened the car door slowly and stepped onto the pavement. She watched me, deathly still, unsure whether to dart or drop mercifully onto the ground. I called to her, easing closer, both of us oblivious to the whir of cars and horns around us. I could sense the adrenaline, hers and mine, pumping in unison. Then suddenly she turned and was instantly back into the ditch, appearing more frightened than before.

Out of the corner of my eye, I saw our son crawling over the seat, half-curious, half-scared, much like the collie. I eased to the car and slowly opened the back door and called to her again in a soft, motherly voice, telling her—promising her—everything would be all right. Instinctively, she must have understood, for ever so gingerly she made her way into our car. Matted and muddy, she laid her head on the cloth seat. Her eyes closed gently and she uttered a long overdue sigh, her breaths magnified in the silence, bringing with her the smell of stagnant water and yesterday's garbage to fill the air. We drove home, each of us silent and unsure of what future we wanted with the creature that lay in the seat behind us.

The next day we called area vets and neighborhood shelters. We tacked up signs and read and reread the Lost and Founds but no descriptions fit. Concerned with her health or lack of, we introduced the scraggly-haired collie to our vet. "Name?" the receptionist asked. We turned to each other and shrugged. "Why not 'Lassie'?" I said, and though we never saw the movie (and still haven't to this day!) "Lassie" she became.

Once the pinworms and the ticks were under control and the round of vaccinations complete, we tackled Lassie's coat, still convincing ourselves the motive was solely for her health. After a number of baths and a shave here and there, the long hairs turned to orderly strands. She was a Cinderella story without the stroke of midnight to ruin her transformation. And what better footman could she have than an adoring eight-year-old boy. Eric brought food and water to rest at her feet for fear she might not find her way to the bowls. At night, he'd awaken and tiptoe down the stairs to make sure she was safe and secure. She got the last kiss on the way to school and the first upon his return. Within days they became inseparable.

Don and I told ourselves it was too early for another dog yet we were content that no one had come to claim her. We were determined to keep her out of our hearts, yet gratefully, we soon realized our hearts were barrier-free.

Today Lassie shares the luxuries of air conditioning and central heat and most of the beds and sofas once she hears the front door close. A thunderstorm brings her quickly to our side, as does a raised voice or a loud noise. Though her water bowl is filled fresh each day, she still has a need for a bit of pond scum in her life and delights in sipping from the backyard bird-bath. Late at night, when she thinks everyone is fast asleep, she slips into the kitchen to eat from her food bowl, probably a left-over survival habit too hard to break.

Lassie literally stumbled into our lives and taught us an important lesson: that love comes in its own time. It's not pre-dictable or preventable. Love is not always a neatly wrapped present on a special day. Love comes when you least expect it and often when you're not prepared. Most importantly, each parcel of love is different, one never meant to replace another, only to add to the fullness, the richness we call life. Best of all, Lassie taught us that anytime is the right time for love.

Editor's Note: Lassie is the dog on the jacket of this book.
Eric is the boy with her.

Old Friends

C. DAVID HAY

Their youthful years have slipped away,
The old man and his dog.
They have a special bonding
That needs no dialogue.

The chase is just a memory,
But how they used to run
When hearts and legs were stronger
And games were such great fun.

Now the pace is slower
For the master and his mate.
If one lags too far behind
The other stops to wait.

Some things we cannot change
Like aging and the weather,
But true friends are quite content
Just growing old together.

from ANIMAL BLESSINGS

ACKNOWLEDGMENTS
(continued from page ii)

"Hero Mom," "Memories With Mitzy" and "A Simple Prayer," by Kathryn Lay, are used by permission of the author.

"Sosha: Therapy Ferret," by Kathy Smith, and "A Tale of Two Kitties," by June Torence, are from *Heart Songs for Animal Lovers,* collected by Hester Mundis. Published by Daybreak Books. Copyright © 1999 Hester Mundis.

"Sweet Shiva," by Robin Kovary, is from *Animals as Teachers & Healers,* by Susan Chernak McElroy. Published by Ballantine Books. Copyright © 1996, 1997 by Susan Chernak McElroy.

"The Kiddos" is from *For the Love of Wild Things,* by Mary Jane Stretch. Published by Stackpole Books and used by permission of the author.

"Bringing Kids Into the Flock," by Dr. Sharon Otis, is from *Pets: part of the family,* May/June 2000.

"Two Strays and a Miracle" and "Klutz" are from *The Compassion of Animals,* by Kristin von Kreisler. Published by Prima Publishing. Copyright © 1997 by Kristin von Kreisler.

"He Had a Job to Do," by Nancy Tomazic, is used by permission of the author.

"The Submarine," by Sharon Huntington, is from *Christian Science Monitor,* September 19, 1996.

"Mockingbird Summer," by Larry Habegger, and "Stop the Car," by Monica Wood, are from *The Gift of Birds,* edited by Larry Habegger and Amy Greimann Carlson. Published by Travelers' Tales. Copyright © 1999 by Travelers' Tales, Inc.

"Peco's Run," by Catherine E. Lord, is used by permission of the author.

"Misty, the Kid Magnet," by Carol Fleischman, is used by permission of the author.

"A Real Star," by Lois Droege and Pam Harden, is from *Boys' Quest,* December 1997.

"Chicken Dreams Can Come True," by Renie Szilak Burghardt, is used by permission of the author.

"Friday: A Mother's Story," by Betty Forbis, and "Friday: A Son's Story," by Scott Forbis, are from *Our Best Friends,* by Michael Capuzzo and Teresa Banik Capuzzo. Published by Bantam Books. Copyright © 1998 by Michael Capuzzo and Teresa Banik Capuzzo.

"Mr. Personality," by Francyne Anderson, is used by permission of the author.

"The Outcast," by Lee Ebler, is from *Country Living,* April 1993.

"The Truth About Snoopy" and "An Answered Prayer," by Christie Craig, are used by permission of the author.

"Everything Happens for a Reason," by Janet Clayton, is used by permission of the author.

"A Time for Love," by Mary Chavoustie, is used by permission of the author.

AN INVITATION TO
OUR READERS

If you would like to share a true story about an animal in your life, we invite you to send it to us. You can e-mail it to: ltta.tripod.com or mail it to LTTA, Box 214, East Greenville, PA 18041.

Some of the stories in this book came from Guideposts readers, just like you, and we welcome your participation in this inspiring series.

A Note From the Editors

This original Guideposts series was created by the Book and Inspirational Media Division of the company that publishes *Guideposts,* a monthly magazine filled with true stories of people's adventures in faith.

Guideposts is available by subscription. All you have to do is write to Guideposts, 39 Seminary Hill Road, Carmel, New York 10512. When you subscribe, each month you can count on receiving exciting new evidence of God's presence, His guidance and His limitless love for all of us.

Guideposts is also available on the Internet by accessing our home page on the World Wide Web at www.guideposts.org. Send prayer requests to our Monday morning Prayer Fellowship. Read stories from recent issues of our magazines, *Guideposts, Angels on Earth, Guideposts for Kids* and *Guideposts for Teens,* and follow our popular book of devotionals, *Daily Guideposts.* Excerpts from some of our best-selling books are also available.